The Arnold and Caroline Rose Monograph Series
of the American Sociological Association

Sociological explanation as translation

Other books in the series

Sociological explanation as translation

Stephen P. Turner

University of South Florida

Cambridge University Press

Cambridge
London   New York   New Rochelle
Melbourne   Sydney

Published by the Press Syndicate of the University of Cambridge
The Pitt Building, Trumpington Street, Cambridge CB2 1RP
32 East 57th Street, New York, NY 10022, USA
296 Beaconsfield Parade, Middle Park, Melbourne 3206, Australia

First published 1980

Printed in the United States of America
Typeset by Jay's Publishers Services, Inc., North Scituate, Mass.
Printed and bound by The Murray Printing Co., Westford, Mass.

Library of Congress Cataloging in Publication Data

Turner, Stephen P   1951–
Sociological explanation as translation.

(The Arnold and Caroline Rose monograph series
of the American Sociological Association)

Includes bibliographical references and index.

1. Sociology. I. Title. II. Series:
Arnold and Caroline Rose monograph series in
sociology.
HM26.T87   301   79-26414
ISBN 0 521 23030 6 hard covers
ISBN 0 521 29773 7 paperback

For my parents

Contents

Preface

The person who attempts to deal with the problem of the explanation of human action must be possessed of more gall than sense, for he must realize that of the many writers who have grappled with it, few have done very well. The origins of the problem must be traced to Hobbes, whose whole project hinged on the idea that a new kind of explanation or means of understanding motions had been revealed by Galileo and could be applied to man's "motions." Hobbes was followed and refined by Locke and Hume and applied to the history of society by Comte, Mill, and Marx. Merely recounting such names shows why these problems cannot be ignored: The writings of these figures on derivative problems of politics constitute the significant political, economic, and social ideas of our time. Because of this, their foundational concerns with the philosophical problems of the understanding of human action remain our problems today.

Curiously, the history of these problems is not widely understood in the disciplines in which social explanations are actually offered, and so scarcely a year passes without the footsteps of Hobbes or of his detractors of earlier centuries being retraced, with the result that a new volume on "theory construction" or "the language of sociology" or "new rules of sociological method" takes its place on an already crowded shelf. If there is any merit to the present work, it is that it is a departure not from the problems of Hobbes and his successors but from the character of their writings. No new explanatory program is offered here. My approach has been to accept the existence and intellectual substance of sociology and to try to show why the substantive problems of concern to sociology are genuine problems and why their solutions are, at least in part, genuine solutions.

I have tried to present fundamental issues in an accessible form by dealing with well-known examples. The analysis of these examples can be applied analogically to other examples of sociological explanation. But I leave these further applications to the reader. The philosophical subtleties of the argument have been made as unobtrusive as possible. The philosophical reader should, however, have no difficulty in relating the argument to ongoing issues in the philosophy of social science. At the technical philosophical level, I have simplified by taking Winch for usufruct: The same points may be stated without reference to his emphasis on "rule following." Apart from this emphasis, the argument may be seen to have an affinity to that of Hilary Putnam's *Meaning and the Moral Sciences* (1978). My treatment of several of these philosophical issues in "Translating Ritual Beliefs" (1979), which does not rely on the concept of rule following, is more closely comparable to Putnam's approach than to Winch's.

Because I do not attempt, in this study, to evaluate the claims of the various sociologies and sociological methods, some readers will reasonably wish to know how I do evaluate them. I have given a critique of both the "causal modeling" and Zetterbergian approaches to "theory construction" in "Getting Clear about the Sign-Rule" (1974). Different critical points about standard quantitative sociologies are made in "Blau's Theory of Differentiation: Is It Explanatory?" (1977), in "Chance and Eminence in Science" (1979, with Daryl Chubin), and in the closing pages of "The Process of Criticism in Interpretive Sociology and History" (1978, with David Carr). This last article is primarily devoted to a critique of the phenomenological approach to action explanation. In "The Critique of Positivist Sociology in Leo Strauss and Jürgen Habermas" (1977, with Regis Factor), I deal with Habermas's critique of the concept of language games as insufficiently transcendental. Symbolic anthropology is discussed in "Translating Ritual Beliefs." For the reader interested in an exhaustive critique of symbolic interactionism and sociological phenomenology from a Wittgensteinian point of view, I recommend David Rubinstein's book on the subject, *Marx and Wittgenstein: Social Praxis and Social Explanation* (forthcoming).

A number of people deserve thanks. Ken Benson and Bill Wilcox provided useful criticisms (and sometimes even more useful expressions of complete incomprehension). My wife, Summer, performed many essential services, great and small. The Rose Monograph Committee and especially its chairman, Robin Williams, showed an important kind of academic integrity in the way they handled a work that they knew would be controversial.

Stephen Turner

1. Introduction: the object of sociological explanation

The great political philosopher Leo Strauss distinguished the modern project in political philosophy from the classical political philosophy of Plato and Aristotle by pointing out that the ancients sought the perfection of the prescientific or ordinary understanding of human things in their philosophy or science, whereas the modern "sciences" of human things, such as sociology, seek to replace this ordinary understanding and are founded on its rejection. Max Weber was Strauss's principal example of this rejection in recent social science. The ordinary person, Strauss pointed out, understands and accounts for the occurrences of political life evaluatively. Weber denied the possibility of rationally evaluating action. In the last analysis, he argued, there are conflicts among various value positions that are irreconcilable by human reason. So, for Weber, scientific knowledge of human action must be non-evaluative and thus radically unlike the prescientific knowledge it replaces. The other classical sociologists reject the prescientific under-standing even more radically than Weber. Durkheim denies that ordi-nary explanations of action can be any guide to the true causes of action. Ordinary concepts are for him Baconian *Idola,* epistemological obstacles to be overcome. Pareto denies the prescientific understanding by dismissing it wholesale. All action that has moral or religious purport is described by him as "non-logical." The true explanations of these actions cannot be the ordinary explanations, which Pareto dismisses as pseudo-explanations, "derivations." They must be sought in deeper causes which, as Pareto characterizes them, are radically unlike the reasons that figure in ordinary explanations.

The sociological project that Weber, Durkheim, and Pareto formed has clearly failed to live up to their expectations. There are neither Durkheimian "laws of the collective consciousness" nor Paretian laws of social equilibrium, and Weber's elaborate constructions of categories for historical causal analysis have not served to give the account of the unique character of Western society that he sought. But the failure is

1

itself perplexing. The less radical diagnoses have suggested that the social sciences simply lack maturity. The proposed cure is time and the amassing of empirical studies and middle-level principles. Yet this diagnosis has been extant at least since John Stuart Mill's *System of Logic,* and the cure has shown few signs of working. The more radical diagnosis places the error at the core of the modern project itself, in the idea of a causal science of man and society that has dominated social and political thought since the advent of the new physics. This diagnosis has its own difficulties. If we formulate the diagnosis positively, it amounts to a claim that the social sciences have been an attempt to apply causal explanatory methods to attain an understanding of that which is already properly understood or can be properly understood by noncausal methods, such as classical teleology and "idealism." This claim in turn depends on an account of these methods. Yet even such a vigorous defender of the methods of classical political philosophy as Leo Strauss concedes that the teleological conceptions of the classics cannot be simply followed today. After the defeat of the teleological conception of the universe, those who followed a teleological conception of man were forced to take up an essentially modern dualism between natural and social science, which constitutes a break with the classics. "An adequate solution to the problem of natural right cannot be found before this basic problem has been solved" (Strauss, 1953:8).

This problem about modes of explanation turns on a more fundamental one, the problem of the object of sociological explanation. The radical diagnosis denies that there is anything that demands any special sort of "sociological" explanation. The less radical diagnosis supposes that there is no special difficulty about the existence and character of this explanatory object; the problem is merely to provide and confirm explanations of the proper form. In this work, I identify one class of explanatory objects and a pattern of sociological explanation that can reasonably claim to include the crucial concerns of sociology. This pattern fits the radical diagnosis in certain crucial respects. It fits Strauss's notion of "the perfection of the prescientific understanding," as the object of explanation arises through ordinary discourse and does not purport to "replace" the prescientific understanding. I also argue, consistently with the radical diagnosis, that these explanatory objects are misconceived as facts that "general theories" of sociology can explain. But the pattern of explanation is quite unlike the sort of explanations or understanding that the radical diagnosis has usually envisioned, because it constitutes a distinctively "sociological" pattern that can be assimilated neither to the model of hermeneutics nor to models of philosophic inquiry, either that of classical political philosophy or that of contemporary "conceptual analysis." The pattern resembles translation more closely than it resembles any other form of explanation or explication. By identifying this class of explanatory objects, I give grounds for rejecting both the radical diagnosis and the conception of sociological explanation that informs Weber, Durkheim, and Pareto.

I proceed by considering the most rigorous application of the radical diagnosis to sociology, formulated by Peter Winch in *The Idea of a Social Science* (1958) and in a later article, "Understanding a Primitive Society" (1964). The appearance that difficulties with explanation take in Winch's writings is often superficially very different from the appearance they take in contemporary American sociology; so it will take a certain amount of effort and perceptiveness on the part of the reader to see their relevance. A similar effort is necessary to see the relevance of these same issues in the forms they have taken in the history of social thought and in the contemporary sociology of the Continent. The effort, however is no greater than and no different from that required to see, for example, the relevance of Habermas's claims to Garfinkel's. The advantages in starting with Winch are compelling. The problems take a relatively tractable form in his writings. Difficulties are not, as is typically the case in the sociological literature, handled in asides. The presentation is explicitly and directly addressed to the difficulties and is developed to the point where a wide range of criticisms can find a foothold.

Winch's position has played a role in British discourse which is roughly analogous to the role that the positions of ethnomethodologists and symbolic interactionists play in North America and which the positions of hermeneutically oriented sociologists and philosophers like Hans-Georg Gadamer and Jürgen Habermas play on the Continent. Winch is opposed to conceiving of social inquiry as an extension into the social world of the methods of investigation and theory construction established in the physical sciences. Like those who have suggested that social inquiry is essentially a hermeneutic study, he takes something akin to "interpretive understanding" to be a logical precondition for sociological explanation.[1] Like the ethnomethodologists, he is concerned with the details of the realization of the "normative order" in action. The parallel to symbolic interactionism has a foundation in commonalities between the rejections of behaviorism in both Mead and Wittgenstein.[2]

Some of the immediately visible differences between Winch's account and these others arise from divergences between the various intellectual traditions in which the various positions developed. Winch writes within a philosophical tradition that is particularly sensitive to the traps these cognate positions often have fallen into: excessive technical jargon, political and moral sentimentalism, and a continuously unfavorable balance of programmatic statements to problem solving. A word about this tradition may serve as prophylaxis against some misunderstanding. Winch writes in the context of what is commonly and misleadingly called "the philosophy of ordinary language." The label is particularly misleading in that it suggests that the philosophy of ordinary language is "about" ordinary language, as the philosophy of science is "about" science. Instead, it is about everything that ordinary language is about: from activities like atonal music to activities like promising. Rather than marking off a subject matter, the name serves to distinguish a body of characteristic philosophical strategies. Where traditional philosophy attempts to answer philosophical questions or explain general features of existence and knowledge by inventing philosophical theories, the philosopher of ordinary language has been concerned to show that these questions result from using words where they do not have any natural application or outside the contexts where they are ordinarily – and intelligibly – used. The popular impression that the philosophy of ordinary language presents a theory of language, it should be noted, is doubly false. The ordinary-language philosopher does not present theories (in any usual sense of "theory"), nor are his remarks about language – at least not in any sense that differs from the sense in which ordinary language is also, on occasion, about language. Accordingly, Winch's conceptual remarks, and the remarks made in the course of this study, should not be read as technical claims within a particular philosophical theory or theory of language (in contrast to the way, to choose an extreme example, Lukács's literary criticisms must be read: as claims within a particular Marxist philosophical system). If the ordinary-language philosopher's distinctions and clarifications make sense, they should make sense on their own account.

This discussion is distinctly not "metatheory" in the usual sense of this term in sociology. Usually "metatheory" has a hypothetical character: It is a kind of prediction of what successful theory in sociology must or may resemble and a prescription to the sociologist that, if his aim is to achieve this particular end, he must adopt certain means. Durkheim's *Rules of Sociological Method* is the classic formulation of this genre and probably remains unequaled in its adeptness in dealing with the many philosophical and logical problems that arise in connection with his metatheoretical hypothesis.

The approach I have taken here is to identify certain philosophical and methodological problems in connection with the claims of theoretical sociology that already exist, and to deal with them not by characterizing them as yet unfulfilled theoretical forms but by showing that sociological explanatory discourse has an intelligible character, a "rationality," so to speak, distinct from the rationality of scientific "theory" that some sociologists take as a model and distinct from the rationality of philosophical "theory" that other sociologists take as a model.

This work is thus not merely another exercise in the deflation of the scientific and theoretical pretensions of sociology. It is in precisely the opposite spirit. It constitutes a defense of sociology as having a legitimate and intelligible explanatory interest apart from these pretensions, and it therefore constitutes an apologia for sociology's genuine achievements in satisfying these interests.

2. Winch's account of the sociological explanation of action

Winch's aim in *The Idea of a Social Science* is to set straight the matter of the relations between philosophy and empirical social inquiry. The view he wishes to correct is the prevalent one in the literature on the subject; in considering the nature of society and the features of particular social relations, this view leaves little of studies in this realm to philosophy, and much to empirical inquiry. The core of his case is a demonstration. He devotes considerable effort to elucidating the concept of "following a rule" and uses the results of this effort to support a number of claims – among them, that actors' concepts must be addressed prior to empirical questions about their actions, and that the nature of questions about actors' concepts constrains subsequent empirical inquiry into their actions in ways that have not generally been understood or acknowledged. It is these claims that are of interest here.

Winch's treatment of rule following is largely taken over from Wittgenstein. The general question that concerns him is this: What is it to follow a rule, such as a computational rule, or to follow a definition, which is a kind of rule about the use of a word? He approaches the problem by looking at a closely related question: What is the difference between someone who is really following a rule and someone who is not? It cannot be merely that the rule follower's actions can be brought under a formula, for any series of action can be brought under some formula or other. Imagine a man A who writes 1 3 5 7 on a blackboard and asks a friend B to continue the series, following the same rule. Almost everyone would write 9 11 13 15. Suppose that A refuses to accept this as the correct continuation, saying that it runs 1 3 5 7 1 1 3 5 7 9 11 13 15 9 11 13 15, and then asks B to continue it from there. B has several alternatives. Say that he chooses one, and that A rejects it as the correct continuation. At some point, after A has refused to accept one continuation after another as the continuation he meant, B

may say, with justification, that A is not really following a rule at all, or at least not a mathematical rule; perhaps he may say that A is really just following the rule of changing his requirements for what constitutes the correct continuation every time one is proposed. And B is justified in saying that A is really not following a mathematical rule, even though there are many formulas A could produce and say, "But you haven't tried the series defined by this one." This brings out one feature of following a rule: For someone to show that he is following a rule, he must show that he is doing something *as a matter of course.*

The same point may be made with a more "sociological" example. Suppose that it was said that in a particular mental institution people were put in one ward or another without regard to their condition, and that this claim was denied by the director of the institution, who said that decisions about where people were placed actually involved abstruse psychiatric distinctions made on the basis of identifiable psychiatric symptoms. To convince you of the validity of this reply he would need to convince you he was following a rule in making diagnoses: that in making these identifications of symptoms and applying these tags to them he was utilizing an acquired skill. You would not, perhaps, demand that his identifications be right all the time—cases might arise where the identification was difficult. However, he would need to show that he could, in some substantial proportion of cases, pick out the particular symptoms as a matter of course. And to be really sure of the director's reply you would have to be able to "get the hang" of the rule for identifying the symptoms yourself.

It is also part of the concept of following a rule that mistakes are distinguishable from correct applications of the rule. Imagine someone using a line as a rule in the following way: He holds a pair of compasses, carries one along the line that is the "rule," and as he moves along alters the opening of the compass, all the while looking intently at the rule as though it determined what he did. Here we might say that the line that serves as the rule seems to *intimate* to him what to do; but it is not a rule, for the notion of following a rule is inseparable from the notion of making a mistake, and here there is nothing that would count as a contravention.

We can see what is at stake here by contrasting rule-following activities to activities that are merely habitual. A paradigm of habitual behavior is the behavior of a dog trained to do a trick on command. There is a right way and a wrong way to do the trick, but only people can apply the criteria. The dog does not recognize that there is a right way and a wrong way and cannot distinguish them; it has acquired only a propensity for behaving in the same way, not a set of criteria for determining what counts as "the same." Contrast this sort of activity to the activity of the student who is learning to copy the natural numbers: 1 2 3 4 . . . If he copies them in random order, we say that he has understood wrongly, and we correct him. What counts as a copy is not given, but a set of criteria for distinguishing what counts as a copy must be learned. The test of whether he has understood the activity of copying the natural numbers (in other words, the test of whether he is following a rule) is not just that he perform the act to our specifications – although that is the test, and the only test, we can apply to the dog. We would also say that a student did not understand copying in this context if he could not distinguish what counted as a copy from a mistaken attempt at a copy. (The test of understanding, however, is *not* whether the student can *formulate* the rule he has learned to apply in distinguishing correct copies from mistaken ones.)

This suggests that the activity of rule following, unlike habitual behavior, is essentially social. Wittgenstein makes this point in another way by considering what would happen if someone had a rule that was "private," in the sense that this person could know with certainty whether it had been correctly applied and other people could not (1958: para. 258). An example of the use of such a rule would be someone keeping a diary of the occurrences of a certain private sensation, E, and following the rule of writing E in the diary on every date the sensation occurred. Wittgenstein asks us to notice what would happen if some doubt arose in this person's mind over whether he was correctly applying the rule (suspecting that he was misidentifying E), or if he came to suspect that at some point in the past he had stopped correctly applying the rule. If such doubts arose over application of a rule that was not claimed to be private in this sense, he could check his own application of the rule by querying other persons. If he was worried about his application of a color word, for example, he might ask an associate a question like "You would call this 'robin's-egg blue,' wouldn't you?" However, he would have no such recourse if the rule was private. He would have to rely on himself to resolve any doubts. But it is clear that any of the means he could use to assure himself would be open to similar doubts. If he endeavored to check his applications of the rule against a second private procedure, his application of this procedure would be equally open to question. How could he know he was applying the second procedure correctly? (If he could assure himself by checking against some public procedure, one of two things would be true. Either the rule could not have been a private one in the first place, or its connection with the public procedure would itself be governed by a private rule – a rule that governed what would count as a check here – and this rule would be open to the same irresolvable doubts about application.)

The lack of a way to check applications is not just a "practical problem." Remember that we established that it was part of the concept of "rule" that right and wrong applications could be distinguished. But look at what happens when we try to apply the notion of "correctness" in this case: The rule follower is unable to describe or indicate, even to himself, the difference between right and wrong. For because there is no way of checking applications, there is no way of distinguishing, for example, a "right" application of the rule from an application that "appears to be right." The fact that here it is conceptually impossible to make this distinction means that here we cannot talk about "right" at all – and consequently it is a mistake to call private rules (like the one on the E sensation) rules at all.

Then why is rule following essentially social? Because we cannot give a coherent account of the use of a rule without mentioning the actions or potential actions of people other than the rule follower. Everywhere we turn in attempting to give such an account we bump up against the necessity of the involvement of other actors.

It would be a mistake to interpret all this to mean that agreement among a group of individuals is all that is necessary for an activity to be a rule-governed activity, as though "the rules" were a matter of opinion that was to be settled. "So you are saying that human agreement decides what is true and what is false? – It is what human beings *say* that is true or false, and they agree in the language they use. That is not agreement in opinions but in form of life" (Wittgenstein, 1958:para. 241). Wittgenstein is saying here that the agreement is not anything that is up for negotiation. If we have both grasped a rule, we agree on its consequences, but we agree on these consequences because they seem to both of us to flow from the rule as a matter of course, because we have both "got the hang of it."

Once he has established these basic features of the concept of following a rule, Winch goes on to make the connection to the concerns of the sociologist. A traditional conception holds that the sociologist is concerned with "subjectively meaningful behavior." The behavior in this category, Weber says, is the "central subject matter" of the kind of sociology he develops, and the category is "decisive for its status as a science" (1947:114–15). It is in terms of behavior in this category that Winch will frame his case. If fundamental difficulties with the "law" account arise with behavior in this category, it would clearly be decisive for its status as an account of explanation in sociology. In this step he establishes one point: Behavior that is subjectively meaningful is, ipso facto, rule governed (1958:52).

One of Weber's key subcategories is action that is oriented "to a system of discrete individual ends (*zweckrational*)" (1947:115). This subcategory includes action in which the actor acts to attain a chosen end and makes a reasoned choice of means. Suppose "that it is said of a certain person, N, that he voted Labour at the last General Election because he thought that a Labour government would be the most likely to preserve industrial peace" (Winch, 1958:45). This is an explanation that cites such a reason. One subjective meaning of the act for the actor, accordingly, is that it is an act which helps to preserve industrial peace.

Notice the sense in which the act must be rule governed if this was indeed the subjective meaning of the act for N. He must take a vote for Labour (in this particular election) as an act that helps to preserve industrial peace. Just as the psychiatrist would need to show us that he was placing patients in a category as a matter of course, N would need to show that he would take the act this way as a matter of course. We would reject his own explanation citing the reason "I wished to help preserve industrial peace" if he did not take the act this way as a matter of course, just as we would reject the psychiatrist's explanation.

What would it be for N to fail to take the act this way as a matter of course (which is to say, to fail to take it this way according to some rule that had the force of "to vote for Labour is to vote for industrial peace")? It might be that N was a Tory and, when asked on other occasions, would use the fact that a person voted Labour as evidence of his *absence* of interest in preserving industrial peace. We could reprove N by pointing out that he had said such things, and we would regard it as an inconsistency – a failure to follow the rule he would have to be following if his explanation "I wished to help preserve industrial peace" were true. When we spotted this inconsistency we might even describe the rule: "But I thought you took a vote for Labour to be a vote for industrial peace!" It would be appropriate to say this even though N had never formulated such a rule, for if he had not been acting in accordance with this rule, his own explanation of his vote would not have made sense. The fact that we naturally say something like this in response to an apparent inconsistency of N's shows that an appeal to this rule, or to a rule like it, is at work in N's explanation.

Now consider what it takes for an observer O to offer this explanation of N's vote. The concepts that occur in the explanation, like "industrial peace" and the rule, which has the force of "A vote for Labour is a vote for industrial peace," must be grasped not only by the observer (who must, of course, grasp the concept and the rule, in order to understand what his own explanation means[1]) but by N as well. An observer O could not very well claim that N has no idea[2] what it is to "preserve industrial peace." Similarly, if N did not identify "a vote for Labour" as "a vote for industrial peace" as a matter of course, the explanation would be wrong, or at least incomplete. We can see this by considering an objection that O' might make to the explanation O gives: "But N said that his neighbor voted Labour, and went on as though this showed that his neighbor was not concerned with industrial peace." The point of this objection is to say that whatever N's desire for industrial peace, he did not follow a rule identifying a vote for Labour as a vote for industrial peace. Notice that this connection between reason and act has the distinguishing mark of a rule connection that was mentioned previously: It is clear what is to count as "the wrong way." In this case, voting Tory is the wrong way to preserve industrial peace.

The category "meaningful behavior" includes behavior that is not, in any clear sense, action for a reason. Weber emphasizes one type of conduct like this, which he describes as "strictly traditional behavior." He says that this behavior "lies very close to the borderline of what can justifiably be called meaningfully oriented action, and [is] indeed often on the other side" (1947:116). We can see why this conduct falls on the borderline by considering it in terms of the concept of rule. Winch says that where traditional behavior is meaningful it is meaningful because it involves a choice: People who choose to behave in traditional ways know what kinds of acts count as a contravention of these ways. This does not mean, of course, that they *deliberate* over this choice. It does mean that the behavior is rule governed. The fact that they distinguish contraventions shows that there is a rule. We show the rule in

the way the actors distinguished contraventions. Some traditional behavior involves no choice in this sense and therefore cannot be called
meaningful.

Meaningful actions that are not "social" under Weber's definition
also are rule governed. Weber gives the example of putting a slip of
paper in a book. What makes this behavior the subjectively meaningful
act of "using a book mark"? By acting with the idea of using the slip
to determine where I will start reading again - acting, in other words, in
a way that represents a regulation of my future behavior, in a way that
commits me to acting in certain ways in the future - I commit myself
to reading from a certain point. This does not mean I *have* to act in this
way. After all, we often fail to fulfill commitments. What distinguishes
them as commitments is that if we do fail to fulfill them, it calls for
some sort of special explanation (e.g., "I forgot," "I tired of the book").
An act can be said to commit me only if this act is the application of a
rule. The connection between my act and the acts I am committed to
is identical to the connection between my writing 1 3 5 7 at one point
in a series and 1,000,001 1,000,003 at a later point. In both cases, I am
acting under the compulsion of a rule.

So what does Winch mean by saying that meaningful action is *ipso
facto* rule-governed? No more than this: In order for an act to mean a
particular thing to an agent - to be an act of a particular kind for him -
it must be governed by a rule, minimally, the rule that identifies the act
as meaning that particular thing and not another, or identifies it as an
act of that particular kind and not another. He does not mean that
people do everything by following precepts, or that for every act it
makes sense to ask for a *statement* of the rule that governed it. On the
contrary, many of the most interesting social rules could never be
stated, but could only be shown. Alan Ryan gives the example of a man
who suddenly announces, "I have got all my usual clothes on," during
lunch in a crowded restaurant (1970:135). Such a person is surely con-
travening a rule of appropriate conduct, but it would be senseless to
ask for a statement of it. This, incidentally, is a point appreciated in
innumerable jokes that hinge on cases where instructions about how to
act are taken too literally.

This identifies the range of contested cases. Winch's next step is to examine conflicts between the features of these cases as revealed in this
discussion and some standard, "law" accounts of the methodology of

the social sciences. He chooses to make his case in terms of the views of John Stuart Mill.

Mill's version of the law account retains the usual elements. "Sociology," he says,

is a deductive science; not, indeed, after the model of geometry, but after that of the more complex physical sciences. It infers the law of each effect from the laws of causation on which that effect depends; not, however, from the law merely of one cause, as in the geometrical method, but by considering all the causes which conjunctly influence the effect, and compounding their laws with one another. Its method, in short, is the Concrete Deductive Method; that of which astronomy furnishes the most perfect, natural philosophy a somewhat less perfect example, and the employment of which, with the adaptations and precautions required by the subject, is beginning to regenerate physiology. [1843:79]

Winch remarks in defense of the choice of Mill as a starting point that these views, though naive, have the virtue of being explicit. He might have also defended this choice by pointing out that Mill was a primary source of insights into methodology for both Weber and Durkheim, and that Mill's conception of the proper strategy for sociology and his arguments in defense of the possibility of a science of society have been repeated innumerable times by subsequent writers, to the degree that their source is now forgotten. One instance of this should serve to bring Mill to the present: It was Mill who advanced the strategy of seeking *axiomata media,* or "theories of the middle range."

Much of Winch's critique of Mill concerns the concept of motivation, a problem that has attracted a considerable amount of philosophical effort (e.g., Peters, 1958; Taylor, 1964). These issues, Winch recognizes, are to some extent independent of the question of the applicability of the law account to sociology. The defender of the applicability of the law account to sociological explanation need feel no compulsion to defend explanations that picture men as machines, for example. He could maintain that explanations must be causal and must appeal to regularities by claiming that the regularities that can be appealed to are those governing behavior under the customs and social institutions of a people, or governing behavior in a species of social institution (like formal organizations).

The claim that explanations can appeal to such generalizations, it should be noted, is by no means a trivial one. It is of considerable importance to any defense of the possibility of a "general theory of society" modeled on the physical sciences. Mill himself recognized this in his writings, though he regarded the study of customs and national character as the subordinate branch of the general social science "most completely in its infancy." He remarks that

> to whoever well considers the matter, it must appear that the laws of national (or collective) character are by far the most important class of sociological laws. In the first place, the character which is formed by any state of social circumstances is in itself the most interesting phenomenon which that state of society can possibly present. Secondly, it is also a fact which enters largely into the production of all the other phenomena. And above all, the character, that is, the opinions, feelings, and habits of the people, though greatly the results of the state of society which precedes them, are also greatly the causes of the state of society which follows them; and are the power by which all those of the circumstances of society which are artificial – laws and customs, for instance – are altogether moulded: customs evidently, laws no less really, either by the direct influence of public sentiment upon the ruling powers, or by the effect which the state of national opinion and feeling has in determining the form of government, and shaping the character of the governors. [1843:91–2]

Clearly, no serious defense of the applicability of the law account in sociology could abandon this "most important class of sociological laws" or the claim that these laws can explain conduct that falls into the category of meaningful action. Winch sets out to show that they should be abandoned.

The kind of demonstration Winch wishes to make is one of incompatibility between two sets of concepts – the concepts belonging to scientific explanation, such as cause and effect and law, which Mill wishes to apply, and the concepts belonging to our normal ways of thinking about social actions, such as reasons, purposes, and rules. Winch begins by pointing out that "a regularity or uniformity is the constant recurrence of the same kind of event on the same kind of occasion; hence statements of uniformities presuppose judgments of identity" (1958: 83). Judgments of identities are cases – indeed, paradigm cases – of acting under the compulsion of a rule. This is easy to see. What is "the same kind of event" or "the same kind of occasion"? How is it that we put an interpretation of the words "the same" in different contexts? It is clear that criteria of "sameness" vary from context to context. We are able to tell that two events or occasions are "of the same kind" only once we have mastered the appropriate set of criteria: mastered them intellectually (so to speak), and mastered their application. In other words, we must learn the rules that govern their application. Where do we learn these rules? The essentially social character of rules has already been established. From what social contexts do the sociologist's rules for determining whether events or occasions are of the same kind come? For the butterfly collector the question of whether two lepidoptera are of the same kind depends on the social context of biology. The criteria are those of biologists and their common activity of biology. The sociologist has two contexts to take into account: that of the common activities of sociological investigation and that of the common activities of the men whom he studies. The men he studies also have rules. It is these rules, Winch claims, that must govern the sociologist's judgments of what is to count as doing the same thing – not rules arising solely through the activities of the sociological community.

This means that the relation of the sociologist to his subject is analogous to the relation between the natural scientist and his peers, rather than to the relation between the natural scientist and his subject. So, Winch says, "even if it is legitimate to speak of one's understanding of a mode of social activity as consisting in a knowledge of regularities, the nature of this knowledge must be very different from the nature of knowledge of physical regularities" (1958:88). The sociologist is not like the engineer, studying the regularities of consumption, output, and wear of a machine; he is like the engineer's apprentice who is learning about engineering – the activity of engineering. This, Winch suggests, is reflected in the commonsense consideration that the historian or sociologist must have some religious sense if he is to understand religion, the historian of art some aesthetic sense if he is to understand art.

Winch makes clear that he does not wish to maintain that the sociologist must stop at the unreflective sort of understanding the engineering apprentice gains of the activity of engineering; but he does wish to say that any understanding which is genuine must presuppose an unreflective understanding of this sort. This means that if the social scientist does use concepts taken, not from the forms of activity being studied, but from the context of his own investigation, his use of these concepts will imply a previous understanding of the concepts that *do* belong to the activity he is studying. Winch chooses the example of the concept of liquidity preference. It is not a concept that ordinarily enters into business life, but it is logically tied to concepts that do enter into business life; and it is only by virtue of this logical link that it is permitted to enter into an account that is a genuine account of *economic* activity. If this link were missing, Winch seems to say, we could not say that the social scientist's account was about (i.e., applicable to) economic activity at all. We would not know quite what it was about, but it would not be about the *acts* of the men that we are trying to understand; for what counts as an act, or an act of a particular type, is dependent on the significance attached to it by the society's participants. An act is an act by virtue of this significance, and any account that fails to preserve this significance must fail to account for the acts *as acts*. Whatever such account could be said to explain, it would not be these acts.

Notice one effect of this. A characteristic activity of natural science is the refinement of the scientist's criteria of identification and techniques of measurement. This activity would simply be excluded from the study of acts. To refine a criterion of identification beyond the level of "refinement" of the criteria used by the actor in guiding his conduct, or to improve measurements to a point where the technique provides sharper distinctions than the actor makes, would not improve our understanding of the acts. It would undermine it, for we would no longer be identifying what the actor is identifying and acting on. What "improvements" we can make are improvements in our *mastery* of the actors' concepts, not improvements on the concepts themselves.

This discussion of the nature of knowledge of "regularities" about social institutions indicates one kind of incompatibility between our normal ways of explaining human conduct and the concepts associated with scientific explanation.

An incompatibility also arises over the links between explanatory factors Mill speaks of – such as opinions, feelings, and sentiments – and acts. These links, presumably, are to be treated as analogous to the relation between two physical events each of which can be identified independently of the other: Whether there is a relation or not is purely a question of contingent fact, to be determined by the investigation of regularities in relations between classes of such acts. But they cannot be treated as purely contingent. The case of militarism is a typical example of what Mill has in mind and shows the peculiarity quite clearly. If a people with what appeared to us to be militaristic sentiments did not act militaristically under *some* range of circumstances, we would not say, "In this culture, the causal relation between militaristic sentiment and militaristic acts does not hold." We would instead say that we had misunderstood what they meant when they said certain things. The remedy for such a misunderstanding is mastery of their concepts, not more refined or precise data; which is to say that the link we seek is a conceptual link, an "internal connection."

Another conflict arises between the notion of prediction that belongs to natural science and the notion of prediction that enters into normal discussions of human conduct. Consider the problem of *O* predicting a decision of *N*'s. He must familiarize himself with *N*'s concepts and his character. But an understanding of his concepts and character, however perfect, is still compatible with *N*'s acting differently from the prediction. This is shown most clearly in cases where *N* is following a particular rule, and markedly new circumstances arise in which the proper application of the rule is not clear; where, in other words, the question arises of *what is involved* in following the rule. In such a case the rule would not specify a determinate outcome, although it would probably limit the range of possible alternatives. Winch's point is that if *O* failed to predict *N*'s conduct correctly in such a situation, we would not take this failure as evidence that *O*'s understanding of *N*, or of the rule, was faulty. We would not automatically conclude that there must have been something wrong with the way he gained his understanding of *N* or with the way he understood *N*. This situation is obviously incompatible with the physical scientist's notion of prediction. A failed physical science prediction always indicates that something was wrong: the method, the calculation, the theory, the physicist's understanding of the theory, or something else of this sort.

Where does this leave us with law accounts like Mill's? Winch has certainly given evidence of differences between our ordinary explanations and understandings of actions, on the one hand, and law explanations and knowledge of regularities, on the other; and he has shown differences between meaningful acts and the objects of causal explanations in the physical sciences. Minimally, these are difficulties a law account must overcome. But how conclusive are they? In a divorce court, a charge of incompatibility (much less, incompatibility to the degree of "irreconcilable differences") is difficult to judge. Perhaps all that should be said here is that we face analogous difficulties in judging this case.

The contrast between mastering another person's concepts and improving concepts in the framework of developing scientific theories and techniques is closely related to another issue, that of the possibility of assessing the "rationality" or "efficacy" of the magical and religious practices of primitive societies. In the case of primitive societies, we are especially tempted to "improve upon" the natives' concepts rather than "improving our mastery," for we react to them as superstitions. In *The*

Idea of a Social Science, Winch objected to this procedure through an examination of Pareto's account of the distinctions between "logical" and "non-logical" conduct, and between "residues" and "derivations." This treatment was not particularly successful (see Baker, 1960, and Bradley, 1960); so he restated his position in a paper treating Evans-Pritchard's account of Zande magic (1964).

In his classic study *Witchcraft, Oracles, and Magic among the Azande,* Evans-Pritchard takes the attitude that, because it has been conclusively shown by scientific methods of investigation that Zande beliefs in the influence and efficacy of witchcraft and magic are mistaken, it is the responsibility of the anthropologist to show how a society can maintain such as system of beliefs. His position is by no means an instance of unsophisticated ethnocentrism: He is quite aware that the scientific understanding which leads him to reject Zande beliefs is a cultural phenomenon, characteristic of contemporary Western societies. Nonetheless, he feels compelled to say, the scientist's belief about magic and witchcraft are "in accord with objective reality," whereas the Zande beliefs are not. It will not do, Evans-Pritchard thinks, to say something like "The savage is thinking mystically and we are thinking scientifically about rainfall," as though the two ways of thinking were merely "different"; rather, we should say, "The social content of savage thought about rainfall is unscientific since it is not in accord with objective reality and may also be mystical where it assumes the existence of suprasensible forces" (quoted in Winch, 1964:308).

Winch points out that here Evans-Pritchard, in his use of the expression "in accord with objective reality," assumes that "reality" must be regarded as intelligible outside and independent of the context of scientific reasoning itself. In Evans-Pritchard's picture, it is by their relations to such an independent item that scientific notions are distinguished. Scientific notions do have the relation, unscientific notions do not. Winch wishes to reject this picture, but he does not wish to lose sight of the fact that men's ideas must be checkable by something independent, some reality; to do so, he says, would plunge us into a Protagorean relativism. Winch notes that our conception of reality is determined by its actual use in language: "We could not in fact distinguish the real from the unreal without understanding the way this distinction operates in the language" (1964:309). Evans-Pritchard is trying to appeal to a conception of reality that is not determined by its actual use in language – he wants something against which *the use itself can be tested.* This cannot be done. We can show the impossibility by asking for the criteria of what constitutes "a true link between ideas and independent reality" (1964:309). It is clear that we would have to draw these criteria from some universe of discourse. If we drew them from science, we would simply beg the question of whether scientific ideas and usage were "truly linked to an independent reality."

Winch draws out the implications of this result by asking if it is in fact the case that Zande magic, like science, constitutes a coherent universe of discourse with an intelligible conception of reality. He points out that by answering this question affirmatively he is not committing himself to a belief in the rationality of all the magical beliefs and practices of primitive men. As Collingwood has remarked, "Savages are no more exempt from folly than civilized men" (quoted in Winch, 1964: 309). Moreover, he is not committing himself to the rationality of magic as practiced by persons of our own culture. For the Zande, witchcraft is part of the foundations of social life. In our culture, these beliefs and practices – for example, the Black Mass and astrology – are for the most part parasitic on our civilization's religious and scientific practices. Winch says that "it is impossible to keep a discussion of the rationality of Black Magic within the bounds of concepts peculiar to them; they have an essential reference to something outside themselves" (1964:310). Hence, when we speak of these practices as being "irrational" and "superstitious," and show them to be irrational in terms of their dependence on our ordinary concepts, we have the weight of our culture behind us, and behind us legitimately. This, in other words, is a context in which the term "irrational" has a proper use.

We are not in this position when we speak of Zande magic; the Zande concepts lack any such essential reference. Consequently, Winch argues, we cannot apply our standards of rationality to their beliefs and practices. Consider the subject of contradictions in the Zande account of the inheritance of witchcraft and their practices in establishing that someone is a witch. The Azande establish witchcraft by a postmortem examination of the intestines for "witchcraft-substance"; they also believe witchcraft to be inherited. As Evans-Pritchard notes:

To our minds it appears evident that if a man is proven a witch the whole of his clan are *ipso facto* witches, since the Zande clan is a group of persons related biologically to one another through the male line. Azande see the sense of this argument but they do not accept its conclusions, and it would involve the whole notion of witchcraft in contradiction were they to do so. [Quoted in Winch, 1964:314]

Contradiction would arise when a few positive postmortem results, scattered throughout the clans, proved every line to be a line of witches, and a few similarly scattered negative results showed every line to be a line of nonwitches.[3] Evans-Pritchard says that "Azande do not perceive the contradiction as we perceive it because they have no theoretical interest in the subject, and those situations in witchcraft do not force the problem upon them" (quoted in Winch, 1964:314). What are we to make of this? Winch suggests that we manufacture the "contradiction" we discover in Zande thought ourselves, that it is an artifact of our treating their views about witchcraft as a system of theoretical assertions whose point resembles that of a scientific theory. He notes that the Azande themselves would not press their ways of thinking about witchcraft to the point where contradiction would arise; and he concludes that it is the European, obsessed with pushing Zande thought where it would not naturally go, who betrays misunderstanding – a misunderstanding of Zande thinking.

Winch is not merely concerned to refute the view that Zande beliefs may be said not to be in accord with an independent reality. He wishes to make the much stronger claim that it is mistake to attempt to treat these beliefs by first showing them not to be in accord with our own scientific understanding and then showing how the Azande take them in such a way, or use them in such restricted contexts, that the peculiarities we immediately recognize do not become manifest to them. This is Evans-Pritchard's procedure once it is stripped of any claim to the effect that Zande beliefs lack the link to an item called "reality" that our own scientific concepts have. An example from *The Idea of a Social Science* might convey something of his view more adequately. Pareto at one point (1963:sect. 863) remarks on the similarity of pagan lustral rites to Christian baptisms. He points out that the rites have a very similar point in both contexts, namely, spiritual purification; but the pagan has a justification for this rite very different from the Christian. Winch says that this comparison destroys the character of baptism as a *social* event. He explains that a Christian would strenuously deny that baptismal rites were "really the same thing" as lustral rites; consequently, when Pareto treats them as though they were, he is inadvertently removing from his subject matter precisely that which gives them sociological interest, namely, the special significance they are accorded in Christian life.

We are still left with the question of what it is to understand a mode of social life. Winch finds Weber's answer to this question close to his own and undertakes to defend it against some famous objections and to correct it in such a way that it is compatible with his own. He first examines the matter of the relation between an "interpretative understanding [*deutend Verstehen*]" of the meaning of a behavior and its "causal explanation," a matter on which Weber himself is notoriously unclear. He is often interpreted as merely recommending the technique of placing oneself in the frame of mind of the historical actor. His critics have argued that such a technique may be useful for the purpose of *discovering* new hypotheses, but that Weber is mistaken in believing that this technique is useful for *confirming* hypotheses.[4] Such critics ordinarily argue that hypotheses with origins in "intuition" must be confirmed independently, by statistical evidence. Weber himself appears to hold the view that *Verstehen* needs to be supplemented with some other technique. Winch argues that neither Weber nor his critics are correct. Statistical data, he argues, could never serve in the evidentiary capacity these views assign to this data; at best, statistical evidence can suggest the need for a better intuitive interpretation, but it can serve neither to confirm nor to refute such an interpretation. For example, if Zande magic is misconstrued as inept science, no amount of statistics collecting could dislodge the misconstrual. In such a case, Winch says, what we need is a philosophical argument, for the problem is really akin to a philosophical one; it is a problem over the point or meaning of what is being said or done. Wittgenstein says something to the effect that the philosopher who gets into trouble over his own concepts is like a savage confronting an alien culture. Winch turns this around: Sociologists who misinterpret an alien culture are like philosophers getting into difficulties over the use of their own concepts.

This sort of argument has many similarities to the Weberianism of such sociologists as Alfred Schutz. Winch separates himself decisively from such views by rejecting Weber's distinction between "meaningful behavior" and "socially meaningful behavior." This distinction is obviously incompatible with the view that a behavior can have meaning only in terms of a rule and that a rule is essentially social – bound to such possibilities as that of the recognition of contraventions by other actors. In the Schutzian picture, the social world is constituted of individuals with the capacity for gaining interpretive understandings of other actors and acting on the basis of these understandings. The starting point for his view of social life is a "study of the meaning-context of motive and the structure of the meaningful within the consciousness of the solitary ego" (Schutz, 1967:45–96). In Winch's picture, understanding itself presupposes social relations between actors operating under the compulsion of the same rules; so it makes no sense to speak of meaning in connection with "the solitary ego," as Schutz does, or of "non-social" meaning, as Weber does.

In a sentence, the Winch thesis is this: The understanding we seek is not in "knowledge of regularities" but in "mastery of rules." This thesis might be stated "mastery of concepts," instead, and this way of formulating it might have avoided some subsequent misinterpretation. However, as Wittgenstein says, "Concept" is a vague concept. We can be more precise about what is to be said about sociology if instead we speak of rules, "rule" meant in the sense of "an employment of a concept" or "a practice." There is another problem with speaking of "concepts." To paraphrase Wittgenstein, it is not in every rule-governed activity that there occurs something one would call a concept. By speaking of "rules" we avoid these difficulties.

Winch proceeded by an examination of the concepts of "rule" and "following a rule." This examination established the social character of rules and the connection between the notion of "rule" and the possibility of distinguishing contraventions. He then made the point that all meaningful behavior (an important category of behavior for sociology) was rule governed, simply by the fact of being meaningful. There must be, at least, a rule that makes the act mean such and such to the actor. This has obvious implications. If we are to understand an act as a meaningful act, we must grasp the actor's rules.

The explanations of action that one may offer on the basis of this kind of understanding are very different from the explanations one would offer on the basis of knowledge of regularities. He wishes to say that the two are incompatible, and because of the incompatibility, the notion that appeals to regularities (in the sense of the regularities of physics) can explain acts *as acts* should be abandoned. An act is an act by virtue of the significance attached to it by the participants in a society. Regularities in the sense of physics are ordinarily developed, refined, and used in such a way that preserving this significance is precluded. This significance is destroyed by the social scientist in another important way. In the study of primitive societies, we are tempted to push native concepts in ways they would not go in the hands of the natives in order to pronounce upon their rationality.

By describing these various ways in which social life is *mis*understood,

Winch makes the case for his alternative, mastering the rules and concepts of a society. He does not elaborate very fully on this view, beyond pointing out its similarities to certain views of Weber's. He stresses that the sociologist can elucidate the concepts that go into an activity, as does the philosopher. Where might these conceptual elucidations lead? What more fundamental understandings might they be a prelude to? Winch never answers these questions at all fully, but in "Understanding a Primitive Society," he drops some interesting hints, which he is careful to label as very tentative. He follows Vico in suggesting that the possibility of understanding human history depends on the inescapable involvement of concepts of birth, death, and sexual relations in all societies. These notions he calls "limiting notions," for they limit and give shape to the understanding of human life current in any society, and those understandings in turn give our lives their significance. Consequently, an understanding of these concepts is likely to play a central role in an understanding of any society, and it is to these concepts that a desire for a more fundamental understanding will drive us.

3. Some criticisms of the Winch thesis

Rather than arguments, most of the critical responses to the Winch thesis have consisted of articulations of intuitive points, each revealing lacunae, or apparent lacunae, in Winch's account. Critics have noted concerns of social scientists that this account will not accommodate, produced examples of occasions when proscribed explanations were appropriate, and suggested alternative construals of the activities of social scientists that would make these activities consistent with his view of the conceptually governed nature of human life but that would put them out of range of his strictures.

These criticisms can be surveyed more readily if they are divided into issue areas. Four areas can be distinguished. There is the question of rules. Critics have pointed out that the sociologist would be foolish to think that the rules his subjects claimed to follow actually guided their behavior. Rules are broken all the time, and the patterns of rule breaking, or deviance, are an important concern for the sociologist. How can the Winch thesis accommodate this (obviously legitimate) interest? Another issue area is "causal explanation." Winch's comments on Mill involve him in the philosophical issue of "reasons and causes," an issue with a very substantial literature. Some kinds of causal explanations of human conduct appear to be deeply imbedded in ordinary usage, and the differences Winch stresses so heavily can be overcome, at least to a certain extent. Moreover, the sociologist's concern with "conditions," like the condition of unemployment, cannot be readily framed within noncausal terms. Another issue area surrounds Winch's denial that activities like witchcraft cannot be judged irrational. To be sure, such judgments have often been premature. Frazer's "chronicle of human folly," *The Golden Bough* (1941), is an imposing reminder of this. But it seems peculiar to conclude that no judgments of rationality can be made. Anthropologists' own disputes over this possibility have resulted in a substantial literature, and much of it pertains to Winch's views. Finally, there are objections to Winch's insistence that the sociologist's concepts must be logically dependent on those of the actor if they are to explain his acts. There are some apparent examples of concepts that sociologists use which are clearly not dependent on those of the people they study, but which cannot be eliminated without at the same time eliminating established, and apparently legitimate, sociological concerns.

The issue of rules and their violation

Alasdair MacIntyre puts the point neatly by quoting a remark of Malinowski's on the limitations of the native informant for the researcher. The sociologist who relies on the native's account of his social practices "obtains at best that lifeless body of laws, regulations, morals and conventionalities which ought to be obeyed, but in reality are often only evaded. For in actual life rules are never entirely conformed to, and it remains as the most difficult but indispensable part of the ethnographer's work, to ascertain the extent and mechanism of the deviation" (quoted in 1973:16). MacIntyre suggests that this is a straightforward conflict: "Malinowski makes a distinction between the rules acknowledged in a given society and the actual behavior of individuals in that society, whereas Winch proclaims the proper object of sociological study to be that behavior precisely as rule-governed" (1973:16). A. R. Louch makes a similar point. He suggests that Winch may be read as urging the sociologist to adopt the naive approach of reading rule books and listening to the rationalizations of the actors he is concerned with. The pitfalls of such an approach need no depiction. Such an understanding of society would be so impoverished that it is in order to wonder what anyone would want with it at all (1963:283;1966:177).

Two responses should be made to this. First, to say that the sociologist's investigations must start with achieving an understanding of the concepts and roles of the forms of activity he treats does not mean that the investigation must end there. Winch says little about the final form the sociologists' account is to take. He is explicitly concerned only with its early stages. This is not to say that his remarks are irrelevant to the final form, but they are relevant only in the sense that his elucidation of the preliminary stages forecloses upon certain possibilities. He is particularly concerned to show that among the foreclosed-upon possibilities is that of a sociology resembling physics.

Second, the notion of "rules" that lurks behind these criticisms is notably different from the concept that plays such an important role in the writings of Wittgenstein and Winch. A comment of MacIntyre's reveals exactly the sense of "rule-governed action" he wishes to impose on Winch. He asks, rhetorically, "If I go for a walk, or smoke a cigarette, are my actions rule-governed in the sense in which my actions in playing chess are rule-governed?" (1967:102). By taking the rules of chess as paradigmatic, MacIntyre is led to speak as though a rule can have only one point: to make an act either obligatory or proscribed. An act in accordance with a rule of obligation or proscription is a rule-governed act. An act in violation is not rule governed, nor is an act that fulfills neither an obligation nor a proscription. This imposition is built upon Winch's insistence that for an act to be rule governed there must be a right way and a wrong way to do it. MacIntyre reads "right" and "wrong" as something akin to "obligatory" and "proscribed"; so he is naturally led to point out that many acts are neither and to express his misgivings about Winch's remark that "all meaningful acts are *ipso facto* rule-governed" by producing the examples of taking a walk and smoking a cigarette. This simply misses the point of Winch's remark, which is to convey the complementarity of the notions of meaning and rule. In order for us all to call an act "meaningful" it must count as something. To "count as something" is to be governed by a rule – the rule that determines what it counts as; whether it is to count, for example, as an insult or a promise, as courageous or as foolish. One of the ways in which acts may count as something is by counting as "obligatory" or "proscribed." But this is certainly not the only way, or even the paradigmatic way, in which acts count as something. There are right ways to act in order to make a threat and wrong ways. But "right" and "wrong" here do not mean "obligatory" or "proscribed." They mean "to count as a threat" and "not to count as a threat."

We can see the misunderstanding clearly in MacIntyre's choice of examples of acts that are apparently not rule governed: going for a walk and smoking a cigarette. The reason we cannot see how these actions are rule governed is that MacIntyre has not provided us with the context in which they can be said to be "meaningful acts." If we fill in the context in such way that they are meaningful acts, the examples lose their appearance of being non-rule governed. Consider the case of a man whose physician has told him that he shows early signs of lung cancer and that it is almost certain to advance if he does not quit smoking immediately. He is still reluctant to quit, and his wife begs him to do so, in consideration of her and their children. He sits before her, coolly lights up a cigarette, and smokes it. We would naturally take this as an insult to the wife. We might say, "It could be meant as nothing but an insult." And it is meant (and taken) this way according to a rule. Moreover, this rule could be of considerable sociological interest. We could imagine a society in which such an act would be taken differently, as an affirmation of masculinity, an act of machismo. We would expect that relations between men and women in a society that followed such a rule would be very different from relations in our own.

Where do these considerations leave the questions raised by the quotation from Malinowski, the behavior that is in violation of acknowledged proscriptions and the question of divergences between professed rules and actual practice? It should be clear that behavior violating proscriptive rules is as rule governed as behavior in accordance with these rules.

When we explain why a criminal act was committed, we appeal to the actor's reasons, motives, and so forth. The connection between these and the act are rule governed. Moreover, a deviant act commits the actor (and others) to future acts. This commitment to future acts is made by virtue of rules. There is a difference between rules like criminal laws and the rules of chess, of course. If you play in violation of a rule of chess, you are no longer playing what can properly be called "chess." If you act in violation of a criminal law, your act does not lose legal meaning. When you commit a criminal act, your future actions become committed under the criminal code, just as your future acts become committed under the civil code when you sign a contract.

These cases are apparently not the ones that critics have found problematic. The cases they are concerned with are ones where professed rules are routinely ignored in actual practice. These cases suggest that Winch's view of the "internal connection" between concepts and action is unsound (opening the door to the claim that actual behavior must be investigated by establishing causal regularities and statistical probabilities). Consider an interesting, and historically important, example of this kind of case: Richard LaPiere's (1934) study showing the divergence between the actual practices of hotels and restaurants in serving Chinese guests and their professed policies. His procedure in the study was this. He traveled around the country with a Chinese couple, seeking accommodations at a large variety of hotels, restaurants, and tourist camps. In all but one of these establishments, the couple was accommodated without incident. Some months later, he wrote to these establishments, asking the question, "Will you accept members of the Chinese race as guests in your establishment?" All this was done with due consideration for a variety of possible confounding effects. In response to his query, over 90 percent replied no. Only one replied yes. The remainder replied that it would depend on the circumstances. To assure that these results did not reflect the experience that these establishments had previously had with LaPiere and his couple, the same queries were sent to establishments that had not been visited. The responses of the establishments that had not been visited did not differ.

A policy is a kind of a rule, obviously, and in this case it appears that it was routinely ignored. In this sense it is a perfect example of the kind of often-evaded lifeless regulations that Malinowski speaks of. However, the example might be used to make a different point: to show how a certain view of policies, norms, conventions, and regulations, such as the policy of excluding Chinese, leads the sociologist so readily to substitute explanations that appeal to causes, statistical probabilities, and suspicious social psychological creations like anticipatory sets and tendencies, predispositions to specific adjustments to designated social situations, and conditioned responses.[1] It is instructive to consider LaPiere's actual purpose in conducting his study, for it shows quite clearly the way in which this substitution has led sociologists to set up their investigations. His purpose was to show that if attitudes were to be understood as "partially integrated habit sets which will become operative under specific circumstances and lead to a particular pattern of adjustment" (i.e., dispositions to behave in certain ways), then verbal responses to a symbolic situation, such as answers to a questionnaire, were an unsatisfactory method of measuring them (1934:230). All that this method could satisfactorily measure would be verbal attitude (i.e., a disposition to say certain things).

But isn't it the case that here we are again misled? By taking the rules of chess as paradigmatic of rules, we are led to take an excessively narrow view of what the policy of excluding Chinese guests amounts to. A closer examination of the policy shows it to be a rather involved bundle of rules. There is apparently an ample stock of "good reasons" for not applying the policy in particular cases. LaPiere suggests several such reasons in passing (though he fails to see their significance): because it would make a scene, because of favorable impressions made by the friendliness and self-confidence of the Chinese, the quality and condition of their clothing, the appearance of their baggage (which, he suggests, hotel clerks set great store by), and their cleanliness and neatness (1934:232). So it appears that in these cases the policy was not applied for particular reasons. And to act for a reason is to act according to a rule (the rule that makes it a reason for that act). It is important to note that the sociologist following Winch's suggestions would not be misled in such a case, because he would be interested in gaining a comprehension of the policy as it was understood by the hotel clerk, exceptions and all. After all, this would be the one relevant to an explanation of his actions. Put another way, because it is likely that the hotel clerks did not find their conduct at all paradoxical,[2] whatever divergence LaPiere discovered between the answers to his queries and the behavior he observed seems to have been created by his imposition of an inappropriate interpretation of the act of responding to a query – interpreting it as a promise to act in a certain way come hell or high water, which it evidently was not.

This is not to say that all cases where professed rules are frequently evaded will turn out, on closer examination, to be instances of the sociologist taking the rule in the wrong way (such as too literally). Sometimes we are in the grip of conflicting rules. Cavell views alienation as an instance of this. He remarks that "what is thought of as 'alienation' is something that occurs *within* moral systems; since these are profoundly haphazard accumulations, it is no surprise that we feel part of some regions of the system and apart from other regions" (1969:26). But here again, the sociologist is compelled to start with moral concepts (and the rules in which they find an application), for this is what an explanation of our alienation goes back to. On other occasions, it is not clear how rules are to apply. Such situations are thought of as "anomic." But here again, we see them as anomic by setting them against the rules that now fail to find their place, not by conducting a search and certifying that no rules are to be found. And to be sure that no rules are operative, we must have a clear view of the rules.

As I have suggested, the LaPiere example can be used to make another point: to show how a certain view of norms, policies, conventions, regulations, and ways of doing things leads the sociologist so readily to substitute explanation that appeals to causal or statistical laws and to dubious mental entities, like "attitude set," and "cognitive systems."

The historical context of LaPiere's study is an interesting one. At

that point in the history of sociology, the study of attitudes was a relatively new concern and was subject to considerable controversy. Its
primary attraction was this: The concept of "attitude" defined a set of
research problems that could be approached with techniques which
appeared to be genuinely scientific, complete with quantitative analysis
and experimental control. An attitude, understood as a disposition to
behave in certain ways in certain situations (or, as LaPiere puts it at one
point, "predisposition to specific adjustment to designated social situations" [1934:230]), is presumably a relatively coherent and stable,
though alterable, property of an individual actor. It is "expressed" in
behavior. The situations in which attitudes express themselves are, of
course, complex; so it would be a mistake to expect more than a statistical relationship between an attitude and specific acts. For the same
reason, it would be a mistake to define a particular attitude too narrowly, in terms of too specific a set of acts, in order to increase the
correlation. On the one hand, to do this exposes the sociologist to the
charge of circularity, a charge that usually takes the form of a methodological objection: that the attitude scale and the measure of the
behavior are "really measuring the same thing." One the other hand, a
concentration on those attitude – action connections where convincingly
high and stable statistical relationships may be discovered has, historically, led to research that no one has found particularly enlightening,
either theoretically or practically.

The set of research problems that the sociopsychological concept of
attitude defines is a large one. One may study the distribution of attitudes or their correlation with other attitudes and with other psychological attributes, like personality type, "tolerance for ambiguity," or
intelligence; the relationship between attitudes and various types of
overt acts; and the relationship of attitudes to previous experiences.
These may be studied by surveys as well as psychological experiments,
and these surveys and experiments may be readily analyzed, using a
large number of statistical techniques. A more phenomenological approach to attitudes is also possible, one that emphasizes the development of attitudes, expectations, and definitions of the situation in
ongoing social interaction.

There is a straightforward theory of explanation implicit in all this
research: Attitudes are explained by social characteristics, by other
attitudes, by psychological attributes, and by experiences; and in turn,
attitudes explain actions and other attitudes.

LaPiere conceived of his research in terms of this theory of explanation. The question "Will you accept members of the Chinese race as guests in your establishment?" was of interest to him not as a question about a *policy*, that is, a bundle of rules applied in a certain way, but as a measure of an attitude, the hotel proprietor's racial attitude. As he puts it, "Nothing could be used as a more accurate index of color prejudice than the admission or non-admission of colored people to hotels." He uses his results to make a methodological point against attitude surveys: "If social attitudes are to be conceptualized as partially integrated habit sets which will become operative under specific circumstances and lead to a particular pattern of adjustment they must, in the main, be derived from a study of humans behaving in actual social situations" and "must not be imputed on the basis of questionnaire data" (1934:237).

The defects in substituting an "attitudinal" pattern of explanation (whether the attitudes are gleaned from questionnaire results or from direct observation) for an ordinary "reasons and purposes" explanation are evident enough. An otherwise comprehensible act, the act of extending service to the Chinese guests, for which there were a number of adequate reasons (e.g., the quality of their luggage), is transformed into a mystery that requires an exotic (and unconvincing) theoretical solution. He is forced into this substitution by his narrow and inappropriate interpretation of the policy of excluding Chinese. It is at the point of taking the policy as a promise to act in a certain way that the mystery is created. If the responses to the written questions are taken as promises, then we are indeed left with a large number of anomalous acts, and it is only natural to seek an extraordinary explanation of them, and even to suppose that "reasons" explanations will be generally misleading and that it is generally necessary to replace these explanations by some other kind of explanation.

The more narrowly we interpret the answers to such questions as "Do you serve Chinese?" the more necessary an alternative type of explanation seems. On the one hand, we induce the sense that the act involves subtleties that only objective, quantitative methods can manage. So we are led to propose and test statistical hypotheses of association among variables representing "actual behavior," "verbal attitude," and various other measurable properties of individuals and situations. Anomalies like the divergence between action and expressed attitude then become statistical variation, to be treated accordingly: as experimental error, by introducing new variables into future hypotheses, or whatever. On the other hand, by our overly narrow interpretation we can make the situation seem highly tentative and mutable and understandable only phenomenologically, or by exhibiting the action as a tentative and mutable element of a developing interactive situation whose outcome is at all points up in the air. Does this interpretation mean to suggest that there is never a place in action explanations for appeals to attitudes, in at least some sense of the word? Not at all. What is being questioned here is the simple "attitude – action" model of explanation that the standard definitions of "attitude" in social psychology are part and parcel of.

The place of causal explanations

The position Winch takes on the incompatibility of explanations of a reason-giving sort with explanations of a causal sort aligns him generally with a variety of recent writers in ethics who have argued that, when we ask why someone did what he did, we are asking for a redescription of the action that "provides an interpretation" for the act or "shows bits of conduct as parts of familiar patterns of action."

The redescription account works like this. We are riding down the highway and you turn off. I ask you,

    1. Why did you turn off here?

and you say,

    2. We are going by the store.

Here the redescription (2), as Anscombe (1957) says, swallows up the act description "you turn off here" that appears in question (1). The descriptions (1) and (2) are different, for the conditions under which they are true differ. The truth of (2) depends on wider circumstances than the truth of "you are turning off here." Here (2) supplies the intention with which (1) was done. Sometimes the redescription includes a characterization of the desirability of the act (isn't this one kind of explanation the attitude model has been used to supplant?) or the object of the act: "Why are we going by this store?" "This store has the coldest beer in town." Such a characterization answers questions about why one wants to perform the act (cf. Anscombe, 1957:68-9). Sometimes we answer "why" questions by supplementing the description with what is commonly called a motive: "Why did you strike him?" "Because I hate him" or "Out of hatred" (isn't this another "attitude"?).

We do not treat such answers as explanations that appeal to causal generalizations, for we could accept the falsehood of any of the generalizations under which the case might fall without therefore rejecting the explanation in the particular case. I might strike a man out of hatred only once, regardless of how many opportunities, the same in all relevant respects, had presented themselves in which I had not (against Ryle). It seems more plausible to view such "motives" explanations as cases of providing an interpretation for the act.

Difficulties with this account arise in the use to which Winch puts it: The disparities between such explanations and causal explanations are treated as incompatibilities, and the incompatibilities are held to debar causal explanations from the context of intentional human conduct entirely. These transitions – from disparity to incompatibility to expulsion – are vulnerable to arguments showing the differences to be merely superficial. Accordingly, the standard philosophical defenses of causal explanation in connection with intentional action have followed a strategy of discerning claims in the form of causal claims lurking behind or concealed within the superficially different kinds of explanations we ordinarily offer or that the social scientist or historian offers. The most famous "act of discernment of concealed claims in causal form," one that has been explicitly relied on by some of Winch's critics (e.g., Jarvie, 1972), is Popper's account of "logic of the situation" explanations in his earlier and very influential *The Poverty of Historicism* (1964). More recently, A. R. Louch (1966:40–9) has discerned a sense of cause more fundamental than the Humean sense of invariant succession of events, a sense from which are derived both the Humean sense and the sense in which the term is used in what he calls "moral evaluations" of actions. A recent, very influential application of the discernment strategy, formulated in direct response to the points Winch makes, has been presented by Alasdair MacIntyre (1967). His account can serve us as a representative of this camp.

MacIntyre points out that an individual who is under the influence of a post-hypnotic suggestion to perform an action not only will perform the action but often will offer apparently good reasons for doing so "while quite unaware of the true cause of the performance" (1967: 100). For example, someone who was acting under a post-hypnotic suggestion to leave the room might, on being asked why he was doing so, sincerely reply that he wanted to get some fresh air. In such a case, MacIntyre claims, we would not accept this answer connecting that reason to his action unless we were convinced of the falsity of the counterfactual conditional statement (1) and the truth of counterfactual conditional statement (2):

1. He would have walked out of the room if no reason for doing so had occurred to him.
2. He would not have walked out of the room if he had not possessed some reason for so doing.

The question of the truth of statement (1) is a question to be decided in terms of experimentally established facts about post-hypnotic suggestion; and these facts, he says, are certainly expressed as causal generalizations. Establishing the truth of the relevant causal generalization would entail establishing the untruth of (2).

Notice what this shows: To establish the truth of such causal generalizations entails the untruth of generalizations about reasons, such as the generalization about reasons that would warrant (2). This has direct consequences for the question whether *the possession of a given reason* may be the cause of an action in precisely the same sense in which hypnotic suggestion may be the cause of an action. Those who have answered this question no, like Winch, have done so on the grounds that the relation of reason to action is internal and conceptual, rather than external and contingent, as causal relations must be. MacIntyre agrees to the claim that the relation between a reason and an action cannot be purely contingent, for this would mean that it would be purely contingent which beliefs are related to which actions (any belief might be the cause of any action), a claim plainly repugnant to common sense. But he points out that *the agent's possession of a given reason* may be a state of affairs identifiable independently of the event of his performance of the action, in which case it does seem as though a reason is an item of a suitable type to figure as a cause, and an act is an item of a suitable type to figure as an effect. Then to ask whether it was the agent's reason that roused him to act is to ask a causal question, the true answer to which depends on what causal generalizations we have been able to establish. Put in another way, he takes this to show that the question is a question of the causal effectiveness of the reason.

So by showing it to be appropriate to ask "Was this reason causally effective?" he has revealed the causal claim lurking behind, and necessary for backing, assertions like "This was the reason he did *x*." MacIntyre points out that one feature of this treatment of the issue is that it concedes Winch's insistence that the starting point of such explanations must be the criteria the agents themselves employ in identifying, describing, and accounting for their own activities. For example, if one claims that the "causally effective" reason for an agent's outrage was a blasphemous remark overheard in a sacred place, the remark must be blasphemous and the place must be sacred by the agent's own criteria of blasphemy and sacredness (cf. Ryan, 1970:153). Nevertheless, the argument does seem to overcome the charge of incompatibility.

The argument, however, has some internal difficulties. Consider a case intermediate to the one MacIntyre describes, a case in which ordinary reasons explanations apply. Several conspirators are meeting in the back room of a bar on the waterfront. One of them, Ernesto, goes out to relieve himself. While he is gone, the secret police burst into the room; drag off the ringleader, Raoul; and leave the others in the charge of Colonel Z. When Ernesto returns, he asks, in surprise, "Why did Raoul leave?" Colonel Z replies, smirking, "He had an urge for some fresh air." What makes the colonel's remark a joke is not its truth or falsity – Raoul may indeed have had an urge for some fresh air. It is a joke because to supply a reason here is a joke, for the circumstances make whatever reasons he possesses quite irrelevant. The question "why" in the sense of "what was his reason" has no application here. The person who asks it has misunderstood the circumstances, and the appropriate response to the question is to set him straight about them. ("I am Colonel Z of the secret police" would, no doubt, have sufficed in this instance.)

The case of the hypnotized subject is not very different. When the subject says that he has an urge for some fresh air it is also a joke, and no less so for the fact that it is an unintentional joke, one that the speaker himself is not in on. This suggests that there is a range of circumstances under which "why" questions, in the sense of "what is his reason," have application. The only persons for whom it makes any sense to pose and answer such questions in situations that fall outside this range are persons who are unaware of the circumstances that place the situation outside the range: in the case of these two incidents, Ernesto and the hypnotized subject. This has direct implications for MacIntyre's conclusions. It suggests that when we reject the hypnotized subject's proffered reason for his conduct, it does not amount, as MacIntyre supposes, to a rejection of the (lurking) claim that this reason is "causally effective." It amounts to a recognition that the circumstances place the situation outside the range in which questions and answers about reasons apply at all. The humor in these situations, such as it is, results from Ernesto and the hypnotized subject proceeding as though the situations were not outside this range. Little amusement could be derived from simple cases of misattribution of causal effectiveness: The humor is grammatical.

MacIntyre's example, then, does not force us to interpret explanations by reasons, motives, and desires as causal explanations. A more natural interpretation of the example is open to us. But the failure of his attempt does not preclude the possibility that we might be compelled to accept such an interpretation on the grounds that suitable ("suitable" here meaning "reconciled with the properties of reasons explanations as they naturally occur") reconstruals of reasons explanations *as* causal explanations would best illuminate both our ordinary manner of speaking about action and the activities of the sociologist. This is a case that is simply yet to be made; in its usual formulations, the sociological aspects of these explanations are left out of account. The possibility of making the case, however, merits a few remarks.

The case for the possibility that our ordinary manner of speaking about action would best be illuminated by a causal reconstrual has traditionally drawn much of its plausibility from the parallelism between singular statements about action, like "He rose because the national anthem was being played," and singular causal statements about physical events, like "The window broke because it was struck by a baseball." There is, however, reason to discount the relevance of this parallelism to this issue.

As Anscombe has observed, Aristotelian philosophy has conferred more terms on ordinary language than any other philosophical view. A certain *façon de parler* about cause is part of this legacy. Aristotle's manner of speaking about cause assimilates the idea of cause to the idea of explanation generally. This assimilation can be readily observed in his categorization of varieties of causes. The list he offers, including material, efficient, formal, and final causes, is a list of varieties of explanation. In view of this historical background, it is at least reasonable to read "because" as "which is explained by the fact that." Other considerations lend credence to this reading. It avoids, for example, the well-known difficulties in interpreting "becauses" that cite goals as cases of appeal to efficient causes (difficulties with which sociologists have become familiar in connection with issues about the logic of functional explanation).[3] What is important to notice is the difference that such a reading makes in relation to the question of the role of cause in the explanation of action: The occurrence of "because" explanations becomes as congenial to one side as to the other.

Hume says that singular causal statements imply causal generalizations, so that if we accept a causal analysis of such statements as "He rose because the national anthem was being played," this seems to have direct implications for sociology. If such causal generalizations about action exist, surely it is (part of) the task of sociology to discover them. And in light of this it is natural to view the activities of the sociologist, such as his attempts to provide a more secure basis for his explanations by trying them out in different contexts, by testing the patterns he discovers against large bodies of data, and so forth, as attempts to move toward these generalizations.

But what would these generalizations be like? A suggestion commonly made during philosophical defenses of causal reconstruals of explanations of action is that we are already in possession of rough generalizations connecting reasons and actions, which have as instances the events the singular causal claims describe; and that these generalizations are, in principle, open to improvement. This suggestion, as Davidson points out, "is delusive . . . What emerges, in the *ex post facto* atmosphere of explanation and justification, as *the* reason" is, to the agent at the time he acts, one consideration among many. Any serious theory of acting out of reasons "must find a way of evaluating the relative force of various desires and beliefs in the matrix of decision; it cannot take as its starting point the refinement of what is to be expected from a single desire" (1963:697). In view of the sociologist's interest, another point against this suggestion is equally telling. Consider a generalization connecting reasons and action like (3):

3. If a girl is born into society *F* and the father reasons that a dowry for the child is beyond the means of the household, he will kill her.

Such a generalization does not settle the kind of question the sociologist asks. On the contrary, it raises that question: What cries out to the sociologist for explanation is the occurrence and nature of the institution of female infanticide the generalization describes.

Now consider a sociological causal formulation that is not vulnerable to the objections Davidson raises because it refers to aggregate patterns, aggregate patterns that result from actions made out of considerations weighed in various social contexts by persons with various character traits, attitudes, and beliefs: the model of the causes of adult status presented by Blau and Duncan in *The American Occupational Structure* (1967). They wish to assess the causal connection between such things as "father's career" and adult status. Notice some features of their formulation: The variables, like father's career, rely on a particular set of local kinship institutions that define paternity in a certain way. The causal relationship, similarly, is a consequence of the fact that participants follow certain practices and customs, adhere to certain beliefs, make certain choices, and the like. The model is a kind of summary picture of this set of local institutions, which lets us focus on certain aggregate aspects. Like the generalization about infanticide in society *F,* it is a *description* of a set of institutions. In fact, institutional facts of this sort are what the sociologist commonly directs his explanations toward. They demand explanation themselves: They are not the end point of explanation.

It is at the point of this explanatory task that the resemblance between these causal generalizations and ordinary causal generalizations begins to end, and the promise of illumination given by the causal interpretation begins to be exhausted. If these descriptions of institutions are causal generalizations, at all, then they are apparently not general laws but are to be taken as what Braithwaite (1953) calls "tendency statements," generalizations with an undefined conditional C under which the generalization is true. The indicated step under this interpretation would be the definition of C. This step presents problems. We can say, for example, that Newton's dynamical laws are true only for physical objects that fall between certain upper and lower size limits, and are false beyond these limits. The laws *may be used* to predict motion for smaller particles and larger bodies, but these predictions will be false. We can, in other words, draw a line distinguishing the conditions under which the laws are true from those under which they are false. We cannot draw the analogous line with formulations like (3) and the assessment of the connection between father's career and adult status. In the case of such formulations there are commonly problems in applying the descriptions under which the predictions are made. In these two cases issues would arise over the application of the descriptive term "father." In a kinship system in which individuals other than the individual who is called "father" in society *F* assume the rights and responsibilities connected with the notions of paternity of society *F,* who are we to call "father" for the purpose of assessing the truth of the putative explanations? The range in which these formulations are true cannot be delineated in the way that Newton's can: Prediction and description go awry together. This means that hypothesized C's cannot be assessed, and such tendency statements can never attain the generality that our institution demands of an explanatory principle.[4]

So the causal law interpretation approaches the limits of its informativeness at a point where the sociologist's interest in action typically begins: with the explanation of conduct under variant institutional forms.

The rationality of other cultures

Winch has been criticized in connection with a manifestation of the problem of the travel-ability of criteria, the so-called problem of rationality. Most of the debate over this problem has been centered on a class of examples drawn from social anthropology, a class largely composed of beliefs and practices of a ritual or magical nature, which are considered "rational" or are held to constitute acceptable grounds for action in the societies in which they occur, but which seem irrational to the contemporary Westerner familiar with "scientific" methods of reasoning. One consequence of Winch's criticism of Evans-Pritchard and Pareto seems to be that the sociologist or social anthropologist is enjoined from explanatory accounts of such beliefs and practices that involve assessments of their rationality.

We are pulled in different ways in the face of this injunction. Crudely, the conflict goes like this. Our first impression is that it is an unnatural and antiscientific restriction. In the course of our inquiries into life within a society, it seems absurd to deny that we can properly say that there are no such things as witches or that we can assess the agricultural efficacy of certain rituals associated with planting or describe the consequences for community health of sanitation taboos. Surely such facts are relevant to our understanding of the workings of the society and the nature of its institutions, and our understanding is more adequate if they are known. Consider how we would respond to a social anthropologist who, in describing the natural setting of a society, spoke about demons as though they were part of the local flora and fauna because the members of the society regarded demons in this way. We would feel misled, and rightly so.

But on second sight, we can see serious questions about the way in which these facts are relevant, about how they are to be formulated, and about how they are to be used. The view that Winch and others have taken, that these facts are entirely irrelevant to the *explanation* of the belief and practices of a society, has behind it the weight of a bitter historical experience. The experience is the failure of Frazer's theory of magic and religion, and the lesson to be learned from it is as perplexing as it is profound. Frazer's error in interpreting magic and religion as inept attempts at the explanation of natural phenomena (of the character of, but inferior in quality to, those of natural science) is not a simple case of bad observation, nor is it an error that can be corrected, in some straightforward way, by additional observational data. Additional data, such as new details about magical methods, could only serve to support an "inept science" interpretation. The mistake that leads Frazer to his conclusions, then, is a mistake made at the beginning of the enterprise, or perhaps structured into it. But what was the mistake? And how can we keep from making similar (though perhaps less glaring) mistakes each time we encounter such beliefs and practices?

Winch understands the mistake to be a case of taking the beliefs and practices (and the talk that relates to them) out of proper context – using them in ways in which they would not be used in the culture in which they are found, drawing implications from them which would not be drawn. Avoiding this mistake and explaining a belief or practice (i.e., a social institution) amount to the same thing: describing the context, the way of life of the culture, in such a way as to make the belief or practice intelligible to us – to show it in its setting of other beliefs and practices and to elucidate the concepts that figure into it.

Much can be (and has been) said in the way of sorting out this conflict. Many of the key terms are used equivocally or ambiguously, and these uses can be distinguished and clarified, as, for example, Stephen Lukes has done with the various senses of "rationality" (1967). But there is a hitch that is apparent without going any further with the sorting out of senses of terms. The hitch is what Hollis (1968) calls "the identification problem," and it works like this. Whether you say that the native's beliefs and the criteria he employs can be judged to be rational or you say that they cannot, it is necessary to identify the beliefs and the criteria in order to say anything about them at all.

He gives the example of certain Yoruba who carry boxes covered with cowrie shells, which they treat with special regard. When asked about the boxes, they apparently reply that the boxes are their heads or souls, and that they are protecting them from witchcraft. Now, is this an interesting fact or merely a bad translation?

If we think of the ways we usually check the adequacy of translations, the difficulty becomes evident: Here the checks apparently do not apply. When we translate something as "The cat is on the mat," we can check this translation by seeing when the phrase is used. We can look and see if the cat is actually on the mat when and only when the cat is described by the phrase. For descriptions or claims associated with ritual beliefs, we cannot look and see.

Hollis chooses to describe this fact in terms that will turn out to raise the original conflict all over again, but his formulation can serve to introduce the problem. He says that what distinguishes the case of the Yoruba belief about souls is that the statement about the cat has "objectively specifiable truth conditions" (1968:232), whereas statements like the Yoruba's do not. When we translate and distinguish correct and incorrect translations of statements like "The cat is on the mat," we have recourse to these conditions.[5] When we translate and distinguish correct and incorrect translations like the Yoruba's, we lack this recourse.

But what alternative recourse do we have? How can the translations of "ritual" statements and the identification of the corresponding beliefs be warranted? The depth of the difficulty may be seen by considering some of the suggestions designed to obviate the problem. We might, for example, translate ritual statements literally, relying on equivalents we have obtained in everyday contexts, and note that the claims are to be taken metaphorically. Hollis points out that this suggestion solves nothing. An utterance may have many metaphorical senses – what checks do we have on our choice of the metaphorical sense to give the result of the literal translation? If we follow this suggestion we are not in much better shape than literary critics interpreting poetry that is incomprehensible when taken literally (and whatever criteria figure into this activity, they are a far cry indeed from those of ordinary translation). More importantly, the identifications of beliefs we could make on the basis of these interpretations would be far from adequate for the purposes of the anthropologist.

This brings out a general difficulty that any account must face: There is nothing to assure us that the senses in which terms are used are not equivocal between ritual and everyday contexts. The same term might take one sense in the one context, another sense in the other.

Perhaps the equivalences the linguist discovers to hold in everyday contexts provide only the most limited clues to meanings in ritual contexts. Everyday logical terms like the "is" of identity, may, in Yoruba ritual contexts, mean the "is" of symbolization. Everyday descriptive terms like "cockatoo" may, in Yoruba ritual contexts, come to stand for a class, such as a class of natural objects.[6] But there is nothing like an independent way of checking such possibilities, and this is what adequate translation would seem to demand.

Winch escapes the main thrust of these difficulties by denying that what Hollis would call "objective truth conditions" are any more than the conditions under which those of us raised in Western scientific culture call something "true," and by asserting that this view of reality is only one among many and in no sense privileged. He pays a high price for this escape, however.

We may appreciate how high this price is by considering the role the idea of "objectively specifiable truth conditions" plays for Hollis. It provides him with the basis for an account of the warrants for translations: A statement p in the language L is true under (objectively specifiable) conditions X, and p may be translated as statement q in language M if q is true under conditions X. Although there are limits to this account in the face of ritual statements, it *is* an account of translation and mistranslation. Winch gives us no account at all. What, for Winch, would constitute grounds for rejecting a translation? What grounds would warrant replacement of one translation by another? How are conflicts between translations to be reconciled? Hollis's formulation shows, at the very least, that these are questions with which any serious account of anthropological understanding must come to terms.

The damage to Winch's account that Hollis causes is indirect: He reveals a lacuna. But the damage is no less serious for that: The lacuna is at least as troublesome as the problem Hollis frames, for its role is the same – one must first identify the beliefs, and first make the translation, in order to explain, no matter what style of explanation one adopts. And what holds for explanation holds for assessments of rationality as well.

Agents' concepts and sociologists' concepts

Winch has also been criticized for remarks on the logical dependence of the sociologist's concepts on the concepts of the actors. His remarks are hedged with a rider to the effect that the student of social life "may find it necessary to use concepts which are not taken from the forms of activity which he is investigating, but which are taken rather from the context of his own investigation" (1958:89). Winch does not elaborate on this, so the target here is not very clear. He could be read as offering a loophole large enough to drive the whole of Parsons through. In an article entitled "In Defence of Sociology," Christopher Bryant interprets Winch as claiming that sociologists cannot "study phenomena which exist independently of any conception men have of them" (1970:99). He counters this with an example: The age structure of a population is a phenomenon sociologists study, and it exists independently of any conception men have of it. One could imagine a society in which age categories were unlike our own or there were no age categories at all. This certainly would not prevent us from studying the age structure of the populations of these societies and discovering principles governing variations in age structures.

Is this really a counterexample? Notice that the age structure of populations of fruit flies, pine trees, or DC-3s may be studied in exactly the same way. The conceptual requirements of such studies are simple. It is necessary to have criteria for identifying members of the population, for counting its members and distinguishing them from one another, and for determining age. In the study of human populations the criteria of the latter two types are biological, not sociological. The criteria for identifying members of populations are many and varied, depending on the purpose of the study. They may be criteria of physical geography (e.g., the population of the southern hemisphere) or genetics (e.g., breeding population x). More typically, they are political, determined by the law of the country studied (e.g., the population of the Republic of Zaire), social (e.g., the population of the clans of the Basoga tribe), or organizational (e.g., the population of the employees of General Motors). In the latter cases, the criteria obviously are taken directly from social actors. When the criteria are strictly those of such disciplines as physical geography or genetics, the claims that are made about the population are claims of these disciplines and not claims for which sociology might be credited. If there are principles to be discovered that use only the terms of these disciplines, they are principles not of sociology but of human biology. In none of these cases are there to be found *sociological* concepts that are independent of the concepts of relevant social actors, and it is such concepts that Winch is evidently concerned to exclude.

Consider a demographic study that supported an explanatory thesis like "The fundamental cause of the economic development problems of Nation X is its high dependency ratio." Notice that the sense of "cause" we encounter here is no different from the sense we encountered in discussing the thesis of *The American Occupational Structure.* It is not a causal connection of the Humean type, but a causal connection that holds by virtue of the following of a number of customs and practices. In this case, these might be customs governing the allocation of labor. Now consider how this explanation might be elaborated or altered in the face of changed circumstances. One might need to alter the description of the customs and practices that figure into it, for these might change. The biological features of the population might undergo relevant changes, and we might need to alter or elaborate its biological description. The natural setting of the society might alter in a relevant way, and this would require us to alter our description of its physical geography. In the face of changes in facts of this latter type, different practices might become relevant to the account, and one might need to elaborate on the description of these practices.

In none of these cases do sociological concepts of the type Winch wishes to exclude enter in, and in none of these cases are the concepts of biology or physical geography used in the ways he finds objectionable: to undercut or replace the categories of the actors. The categories of the actors retain their front-and-center place in the account, in the description of the customs and practices in virtue of which the causal connection holds. Can the thesis "The fundamental cause of the economic development problems of nation X is its high dependency ratio" be assimilated to Winch's views? If we recognize that the connection here is not causal in the Humean sense, because it holds by virtue of the following of certain customs, and if we accept Winch's view of the kind of explanation appropriate to the study of customs, no conflict need arise. It is only when such explanations purport to consist entirely of causal connections logically independent of the following of particular sets of customs that any conflict arises.

Where does this leave us with the Winch account? Two of these issue areas, the concept of "rules" and the use of concepts like "age structure," resolved into matters requiring only additional explications of Winch's remarks. The difficulties over rules arose from taking a too narrow view of "rule." Winch does not suggest that the sociologist's interest is restricted to what can be looked up in rule books or in the rules the members of a society profess to follow. Deviant acts are not excluded from consideration, either. Rules of identification are required, after all, to distinguish "real" violations of norms or laws, and these identifications impose, by rule, obligations on others. The difficulties over "age structure" were resolved by showing that the concept of age structure was not, as it first appeared to be, a counter-example to Winch's claims about sociological concepts. The criteria that the concept of age structure relied upon turned out either to be nonsociological, drawn from such disciplines as biology, or to depend on the concepts of actors, in the Winchean sense.

The other two issue areas resolved into serious difficulties. The problems over reasons and causes backed into the same corner both law formulations of reasons explanations and accounts that construe formulations of the Blau–Duncan occupational-structure type. The difficulties arise when we go to turn these formulations into general, and hence explanatory, laws. We discover that descriptions under which predictions and explanations are made do not readily apply outside certain social contexts. So we find it impossible to distinguish contexts under which the formulations are true from contexts under which the formulations are false; and this makes it impossible to formulate conditionals in entirely general terms that define the range under which the formulation is true. We are left with conditionals like "in society X," which are clearly not general; and under the standard view of explanation, such nongeneral formulations are not explanatory. Noncausal accounts of the explanation of action are immune to difficulties of this nature, but only to the extent that they do not claim to offer explanations across social contexts. When they do make such claims, parallel problems arise: A redescription in the actor's conceptual terms is intelligible only to those who share the actor's concepts. In this sense, such accounts are backed into the same corner, though in a different way.

Offering explanations across vastly different social contexts is a large part of the business of sociology. The difficulties appear most acutely in connection with the explanation of ritual practices and beliefs in nonliterate societies. It is necessary for any account of the explanation of these beliefs to face up to the problem of translating them, for the explanations are to be offered to literate scholars, not to the natives. Winch does not face up to it, and the difficulties are such that no direct extension of his views would overcome them. This backs him even more firmly into the corner of trouble with comparisons across social contexts.

4. A pattern of explanation

The corner of difficulties with applying concepts across social contexts is a crowded one indeed. Winch, the law account of reasons explanations, and those attempting to turn formulations of the Blau–Duncan occupational-structure type into general laws all get backed into it in one way or another. Is there a way out? The obvious place to look first is to the explanatory activities of comparative sociology, for here particular problems with divergent concepts arise and are dealt with.

In what follows, I examine two cases of comparative explanation in which problems of conceptual divergence are central. One is taken from the sociology of nonliterate societies and the other is taken from political sociology. What has preceded, the statement of Winch's case and the discussion of the criticisms raised against it, sets the issues with which the examination will be concerned. By bringing out features of these two cases as explanations, it is intended that a way will be shown to untie the knots Winch ties, while leaving unraveled what Winch has successfully unraveled. The examination focuses on the idea of sociological puzzles arising from comparisons and on the resolution of the puzzles.

A few cautionary remarks might serve to prevent some misunderstanding of what is attempted here. The central purpose of this chapter is to identify a pattern of explanation. My concern in the discussion of each of these examples is to exhibit features of the argumentation. Needless to say, the authors of these examples have methodological and philosophical fires of their own to fuel, and would describe their intentions in offering various arguments in ways other than those set out here. Because the point is to see these arguments in new ways, these differences are to be expected. Put differently, the intentional fallacy can be as much an obstacle to understanding in the philosophy of science as it is in literature. For our purposes, it is the explanatory force and rational basis of the arguments that need assessing. We should not let the labels placed on the arguments by their authors distract us.

The imperative of seeing through vagaries of formulation and style has led to an unintended, but unsurprising, pattern in the choice of cases. Both are patently sociological studies. Yet neither of their authors is a professional sociologist. The reason that such studies might be more attractive for purposes like mine is apparent. The structure of these analyses is more readily accessible than it would be if the authors were adhering to the stylistic rituals of contemporary professional sociology, which, as Chomsky puts it, reflect the discipline's attempts "at mimicking the surface features of the natural sciences" (1968:v).

Exemplars are, first, pedagogical aids; if we are interested in teaching a new way of seeing familiar examples, we are often compelled to start with examples that do not lend themselves so readily to the old way of seeing. It might also be added that the choice of examples should not be construed as an implied affirmation of their "truth." Just as features of explanatory reasoning and argumentation in astrophysics can be illuminated by considering controversies and positions now recognized to be mistaken or currently in dispute, examples of sociological reasoning whose merits are now unsettled can serve to illustrate various rational considerations.

A final terminological point: In this chapter, I use the term "practice" instead of "rule." I mean, however, the same thing that Wittgenstein and Winch mean when they talk about the concept of rule and following a rule. The substitution is designed to avoid the natural reaction of many sociologists to read "rule" as "explicitly stated norm," which serves only to distract from the point of what is said. The term "practice" is more suggestive of "acquired skill," which is closer to the mark.

What sort of answer can we give to the question "What goes on when we offer comparative explanations in sociology?" We may begin by looking at the activity of comparing games, and asking, "What goes on in this activity?" In *Remarks on the Foundations of Mathematics* (II, para. 14), Wittgenstein answers in this way:

How do we compare games? By describing them – by describing one as a variation of another – by describing them and *emphasizing* their differences and analogies.

"In draughts there isn't a rook" – what does this mean? (It sounds childish.) Does it only mean that none of the pieces in draughts is called "rook"; and if we did call one of the pieces that, would there be a rook in draughts? But what about *this* proposition: "In draughts all the pieces have the same powers, but not in chess"? Whom am I telling this? Someone who already knows both games, or someone who does not yet know them. Here it looks as if the first one stands in no need of our information and the second can do nothing with it. But suppose I were to say: "See! In draughts all the pieces have the same powers, . . ." or better still: "See! In these games all the pieces have the same powers, in those not." But what does such a proposition do? It introduces a new *concept,* a new ground of classification. I teach you to answer the question: "Name games of the first sort" etc. But in a similar way it would be possible to set questions like: "Invent a game with a rook." [1956:61]

We can immediately recognize similarities to the comparisons the sociologist makes. The game comparer can "invent a game with a rook," the sociologist can conceive of a society with electoral institutions – or a society without them. As the game inventor can give the participants different powers or pieces with different powers, the sociologist can consider questions about societies or social arrangements in which participants have different capabilities to act in various ways. The sociologist, like the game comparer, may form propositions about these differences that introduce new concepts. In one society, actors identify themselves as members of named groups and marry only within these groups; in another society, such identifications are not made. When we give an account of some difference between these two societies, we might need to refer to this fact; we can name the practice of making such identifications; and we may apply the concept to other societies. The concept, the new ground for classification, need not enter into the life of any of the societies we are describing by this name. As M. Jourdain discovered that he was speaking prose, we may discover that our own society is of this type or that type. We do not need a concept of prose to speak prose, nor do we need a concept of "caste system" to live a life in accordance with the rules of such a system. These concepts belong to the activity of comparing, not to the activities themselves. In this chapter we put these similarities to work.

Consider an example of a controversy where the issue of translation and the identification of beliefs figure prominently. In *North Queensland Ethnographic Bulletin* 5, W. E. Roth published this description of certain beliefs of the Tully River Blacks:

A woman begets children because (a) she has been sitting over the fire on which she has roasted a particular species of black bream, which must have been given to her by the prospective father, (b) she has purposely gone a-hunting and caught a certain kind of bullfrog, (c) some men may have told her to be in an interesting condition, or (d) she may dream of having the child put inside her. [Quoted in Leach, 1969: 87]

He took this to mean that his informants were ignorant of any causal connection between copulation and pregnancy. The report was later used by James Frazer in connection with the thesis that certain "tales of virgin mothers are relics of an age of childish ignorance when men had not yet recognized the intercourse of the sexes as the true cause of offspring" (1941:347). In the sixties the issue was revived by Melford F. Spiro in response to a remark of Edmund Leach denying that this report should be interpreted as evidence for the assertion "that these Australian aborigines were ignorant of the connection between copulation and pregnancy" (Leach, 1969:87). Leach suggests that the report indicates rather that in this society "the relationship between the woman's child and the clansman of the woman's husband stems from public recognition of the bonds of marriage, rather than from the fact of cohabitation." Against this interpretation, Spiro points out that only two of the four beliefs have reference to a male, and they are left unexplained by Leach's interpretation. He argues that additional evidence is required to prove that the remaining two beliefs mean what Leach claims they mean. He asks if this is

the interpretation which the aborigines place on these beliefs? There is certainly no evidence for this assumption. Perhaps, then, this is the meaning which they intended to convey, even though they did not do so explicitly? But even if we were to grant that, for some strange reason, aborigines prefer to express structural relationships by means of biological symbolism, how do we *know* that this was their intention? Perhaps, then, the symbolism is unconscious, and the structural meaning which Leach claims for these beliefs, although intentional, is latent? This interpretation is certainly congenial to other "modern interpretations." Again, however, we are hung up on the problem of evidence. From what ethnographic data, or from what psychological theory of the unconscious, can this meaning be inferred? If, then, there is no way of *demonstrating* that either the manifest or the latent content of these symbols has reference to the structural relationship between a woman's children and the clansmen of her husband, I am compelled to discard this interpretation as not only implausible but false. I shall insist, instead, that the aborigines are indeed ignorant of physiological paternity, and that the four statements quoted in Roth are in fact proffered explanations for conception. [1966:111–12]

Leach has responded rather elaborately, and it is his response that is of interest. Spiro, he first points out, supposes that to identify correctly the ritual beliefs, dogmas, or orthodoxies that are described when an ethnographic report says, "The members of tribe X believe that . . . ," it is necessary to show that these ritual beliefs must somehow correspond to an inner psychological attitude of the actors. As Spiro rhetorically asks, "How do we *know* that this was their intention?" The statements, Spiro says, are prima facie for the purpose of explaining pregnancies. To show otherwise would be to show that the users' purposes were otherwise. Because Leach has not provided any evidence of their intentions, either conscious or unconscious, Spiro finds his claims unconvincing. Leach undercuts Spiro's objection by showing the statements at issue to be of another type – not explanations, but statements of dogma. For such statements, Leach wishes to show, Spiro's questions and demands for this kind of evidence are irrelevant.

Leach proceeds by offering a series of comparisons to statements and ritual acts that, as we recognize, do not require evidence of the intentions or purposes of the actors in order to be interpreted. We recognize this because the statements or ritual acts are those of our own culture. His first sortie at the issue of purpose and intention consists of a comparison to marriage customs of English societies. He points out that many English girls go through the ritual of a Church of England marriage service, in which the groom gives the bride a ring, a priest lectures her on the importance of childbearing, and she has rice poured over her head (a ceremony, Leach remarks, roughly analogous to those of the Tully River Blacks). The mere fact that she goes through these performances tells us little about what the girl knows or feels, her purposes or intentions. She may have chosen to go through a church ceremony for any number of reasons with any number of beliefs or intentions. She may be an atheist, believe that the well-being of future children depends on a church wedding, or whatever. We cannot even infer much knowledge of the ritual itself. Leach points out: "These rituals are, as it happens, structured in an extremely clear and well-defined way, but not one bride in a thousand has even an inkling of the total pattern" (Leach, 1969:120). He develops this comparison between the religious dogmas behind the rituals of our own kinship system and the beliefs reported by Roth.

His next step is to cast doubt on some supports of Spiro's interpretation. He first reviews the classical objections. When we compare the views of the Tully River Blacks about the causal connection between copulation and pregnancy in animals to their claims about men, we find an odd disparity. Roth records that they freely admit the causal connection in animals other than man. This observation suggests, Leach concludes, that theirs is not ignorance of the facts of physiological paternity "in any simple sense."

The reason this fact is of significance is that it weighs against the implicit Frazerian comparison of the beliefs of the savage to those of an ignorant child of our own culture and against similar comparisons. In our own culture's explanations of biological phenomena, no such disparity exists. We make the transition back and forth between explanations of human biology and explanations of the biology of other animals quite readily. When a child learns a technique of explaining a biological fact about animals other than man, such as the fact of the connection between copulation and pregnancy, we expect that the child will be perfectly capable of applying the technique of explanation to humans, if it occurs to him to do so. One is reminded of the old joke about the boy who is left on the farm with the instructions "If anyone calls while we're gone, tell him I charge five dollars for the red bull and ten dollars for the black bull." An irate man shortly comes to the door and announces, "Herman got my daughter pregnant!" To this the boy replies, "The red bull costs five dollars and the black bull costs ten dollars, but I don't know how much he charges for Herman." Our expectation that the child can make this transition seems to explain why, in our culture, discussions of animal sexuality are, for the most part, taboo in the same contexts in which discussions of human sexuality are taboo. If we were to accept the implicit comparison to children of our own culture, we would have to swallow the notion that the Tully River Blacks, who show their intellectual competence in their technical sophistication, somehow overlook the possibility of applying the explanation to humans. This is conceivable, but not very likely.

The fact they they do not make the transition suggests that they take questions about human conception differently from questions about animal conception. The second classical objection points to an alternative set of comparisons that indicates what the nature of this difference might be. When the account given by the Tully River Blacks of how *ordinary* human births occur is compared to accounts of the magical conception of mythological heroes from all over the world, we discover very strong resemblances.

Leach sets out to show these comparisons to be the appropriate ones. He argues that the Tully River Blacks placed the questions Roth asked in a ritual context, and answered accordingly. He relies on ethnographic material about related Australian groups to show some of the ways the details of the setting might be filled in. He then shows this ritual belief to be a variant of the ritual beliefs with which we are already familiar. To support the view that, when the Tully River natives make the transition from explaining animal pregnancies to explaining human pregnancies, they are also making a transition to a ritual context, he cites an intermediate case: one with resemblances on one side to the typical case, where human conception is explained in the same context, and with resemblances on the other side to the case where human conception is described solely in ritual terms. According to Meggit the answer one gets from a Walbiri to questions about conception depend on who is asked and what the circumstances are: "In ritual contexts, men speak of the action of the *gurawari* (spirit entities) as the significant factor; in secular contexts they nominate both the *gurawari* and sexual intercourse. The women, having few ritual attitudes, generally emphasize copulation" (quoted in Leach, 1969:90).

The disanalogy to the Walbiri case is in the way in which the doctrine is held. For the Walbiri, the two kinds of explanation coexist. In one set of contexts, one sort is offered; in another set of contexts, the other. For the Tully River Blacks the denial of a male contribution appears to be a kind of dogma. Leach suggests that the Tully River Blacks were able to persuade Roth that they were ignorant of physiological paternity because the belief was maintained as a dogma, just as Catholics maintain the virgin birth of Jesus as a dogma. It no more needs to indicate *ignorance* in the one case than in the other.

There are other analogies to the Christian doctrine. The denial of St. Joseph's physiological contribution goes hand in hand with an affirmation of his sociological paternity. St. Matthew and St. Luke affirm the virgin birth (or at least have been read to), but they still place Jesus in a direct line of descent *through* Joseph. Leach remarks: "In other words, the kind of interpretation which I put on Roth's evidence and which Professor Spiro finds so novel and unacceptable has been orthodox among Christians for about 1,600 years" (1969:96). Where do the explanations Roth describes (roasting the species of Black bream, catching a certain kind of bullfrog, being told to be in an interesting condition, dreaming of having the child put inside her) fit in? Leach's suggestion is that Roth's informants were describing signs or heralds of pregnancy, not causes. Notice how the ritual is used. The first two occurrences are ways in which a woman may announce her pregnancy. The second two we can see as annunciations of the same sort as the annunciation to the Holy Mother. The woman may report the second two occurrences and thereby also use them to announce the fact of pregnancy.

The connection between particular problems of translation and particular problems of explanation is often intimate. The kinship between the concept of explanation and that of translation in some contexts is close as well. Consider two statements about the difficulties of diplomats in explaining Watergate developments. This one was taken from a national news magazine:

"One of the biggest problems we have," sighed a European diplomat, "is trying to translate the internal politics of one country into the language of another. It's almost impossible to explain the intricacies of what is happening here."

An alternative that transposes the two terms, like

"One of the biggest problems we have," sighed a European diplomat, "is trying to explain the internal politics of one country in the language of another. It's almost impossible to translate the intricacies of what is happening here,"

reads just as naturally, and the rephrasing does not alter the meaning. Both the conceptual and practical aspects of this relation between the two activities may be seen quite clearly in the Spiro–Leach dispute.

Viewed in one way, the issue is an issue of translation with ramifications of the type Hollis describes. Spiro assumes a translation that would run something like this:

When they say such and such (about the causes of pregnancy) they mean what a person innocent of understanding (like a child) would mean if he said that the causes of pregnancy were dreams, catching frogs, etc.

Leach's translation would run something like this:

When they say such and such (about the causes of pregnancy) they mean what a devout Roman Catholic means when he says that the conception of Jesus was caused by God without any male contribution, and by "cause" they mean what the Roman Catholic would mean if he pointed to signs of this divine act (like the annunciation).

Roughly, an adequate translation would yield us claims that had the same implications in both languages. The root issue between Spiro and Leach is whether the assertion of these claims has a particular implication: that the actor who makes the claim is ignorant of physiological paternity. If we translate the claim as an ordinary explanation of a natural phenomenon, governed by the same rational considerations and evidentiary requirements as other explanations of natural phenomena, it does imply ignorance. If, alternatively, these claims are part of a religious ideology, a species of the dogma of the virgin birth, it does not imply ignorance. There is a substantial difference between the two versions, substantial enough for Spiro to find Leach's false and to ask how we could ever know or demonstrate the truth of such interpretations.

We can see in Spiro's remarks the embryonic form of Hollis's conclusion that translations of ritual beliefs are uncheckable. Unlike Hollis, however, Spiro does not simply throw up his hands in the face of these difficulties. He enters specific requests for certain kinds of evidence: evidence about the way the Tully River natives intend the claims to be understood, or, in place of this, evidence of their unconscious "symbolic" intent.

Leach's response is to produce evidence that undercuts the analogy between these claims and ordinary expectations of natural phenomena on which Spiro's translation relies, and to support his own translation by elaborating the analogies between these claims and religious ideologies. He shows that the uses of these claims more closely resemble the uses of religious dogmas than the uses of scientific claims. They are, for example, held as a kind of dogma rather than as a kind of scientific or technical hypothesis that is open to ordinary discussion. This answer serves to annul the questions of intent Spiro raises. If it is a dogma or ritual belief, evidence of intentions is largely irrelevant to *questions of interpretation.* The intentions of the actors may be as varied as the intentions of participants in Church of England marriage rituals, and evidence of their intentions is just as irrelevant to the interpretation of these rituals as evidence of the intentions of members of wedding parties.

Viewed in another way, the issue between Spiro and Leach is a sociological matter. Spiro's translation commits him to asking certain kinds of questions, namely, questions designed to yield an explanation of the Tully River natives' adherence to a wrong explanation of a natural phenomenon. People do, of course, commonly hold wrong views about facts of nature, and the strategies for explaining how they could manage to do so are not mysterious. If we are told that "the medievals thought the earth flat," we explain it by describing a situation in which this is a reasonable or justified belief. We cite facts of which we are aware and they were not, like "Magellan had not made his voyage, so they did not know that it was possible to circumnavigate the globe." Sometimes this sort of explanation suffices, but often it leaves other issues unsettled, like questions about the relation of this belief to other beliefs or various practices, or about the bent of their thought, which are things we might need to appeal to if, for example, religious panics were provoked by new discoveries. Often, as well, there are no "facts," like that of Magellan's voyage, to be cited. We may try to work our way back up the chain of reasons and justifications and find that their ways of reasoning and justifying are themselves opaque to us. Sometimes we explain by describing the world view that the belief is part of (and in terms of which the belief is reasonable or justified). Here we mark an end to the chain of reasons and justifications, for there are no "reasons" for or "justifications" of world views. Sometimes the mistaken belief is part of a body of practice, and its only "justification" is the face one of its actual practical application. Here we describe the body of practice and show the practical necessity or warrant of the belief or describe the practical consequences of a failure to follow those customs that present themselves to the practitioner. Spiro's explanation of the belief – that the physiological connection had not yet been recognized by the aborigines – is simple, but it has a wide range of implications for other beliefs and social practices. These implications, we shall see, are ones that Leach will concern himself with explaining when he advances his alternative account.

Leach's translation commits him to a different question: not "Why this mistaken belief?" but "Why this dogma?" Such a question may be answered using essentially the same means available in the case of mistaken beliefs. However, because of the different characters of religious ideology and bodies of practical knowledge (differences indicated in the Christian theologian's remark that there are different kinds of truth, these same means lead the explanations in other directions. A question like "Why this religious ideology?" is likely to lead us straight to the portrayal of world views or to the description of the customs and practices of social organization that the ideology may be used to defend or rationalize. For explanations of this sort, the going, needless to say, will typically be difficult.

It is common to summarize the strategies for explaining dogmas and beliefs under some formula like "describing the beliefs or institutions in their setting" or "bringing out features of the context." The formula is accurate as far as it goes. These explanations are indeed descriptions of "setting" and "context." But obviously there is much more to be said. What makes something count as part of the context? What distinguishes relevant parts of the setting from irrelevant parts? How much context needs describing for a given explanation? What makes a description of the context the appropriate description, and what justifications may be advanced for it? In short, though it is true enough that we describe the context, when we offer such explanations, the description must be of a certain kind and do certain things.

In the case of translation, taking a wider look around is a step in a certain process. We start with a puzzle of the form "Where they say x, what do we say?" and hypothesize a rule like "Where they say x, we say y." This rule formulates an analogy between the use of x in the one language and the use of y in the other. We may discover that the hypothesized rule leads us astray on certain occasions of the use of x: We draw wrong conclusions, or cannot make ourselves understood. This gives us a puzzle of the form "Why did the rule work (or appear to work) on this occasion and not on that one?" It is at this point that we must do the looking around at the setting. We are looking for something specific: material, like conduct, expressions used in connection with x, and so forth, with which to construct analogies between the "game" or set of usages of which the expression is a part and such sets in our own language. Our goal will be to find a rule, or an analogy, that will not break down, as our first hypothesized rule did.

When we are doing comparative sociology, the process is parallel. We proceed as though we hypothesized that *where we (or another group) would follow such and such a rule or practice, or act in such and such a way given some reason, they (or some other group) would do the same.* I will call this the "same-practices hypothesis." The puzzles arise when this hypothesis breaks down or appears to break down. Not uncommonly, ascertaining whether there really is a breakdown and identifying the place where it occurs constitutes the bulk of the sociologist's task in offering a comparative explanation. We must ask whether it is really a breakdown, or whether we are making a misapplication of the hypothesis. We may, for example, fail to recognize a practice of ours in a practice of theirs. Early European travelers in Africa came back with all manner of reports to the effect that the natives had no language, or no religion. Today sociologists argue such questions as "Is there a culture of poverty?" There are apparent differences in the life-style and conduct of the poor, some of which seem to perpetuate their poverty. To ask whether there is a culture of poverty is to ask if these differences are the result of poor people's following (under radically less favorable circumstances) substantially the same customs and practices, and pursuing substantially the same goals and reasonings, as the nonpoor, or to ask if they are the result of different customs, practices, reasons for acting, and choices. The problem here is to discern the practices of the nonpoor in the practices of people living under the radically different circumstance of poverty or to recognize language in the noisemaking of the traveler's Africans and religion in their ceremonies. If there is a "culture of poverty," if a "breakdown" in the same-practices hypothesis can be shown, the sociologist sets the explanatory task of accounting for this culture. If the apparent breakdown of the same-practice hypothesis is shown to be a result of its misapplication – a result, for example, of a failure to recognize the practices of the nonpoor in those of the poor because of the differences in circumstances – we have an entirely different explanatory problem.

The Spiro–Leach case provides an excellent illustration of the process of setting, rejecting, and replacing puzzles, as well as examples of the kinds of grounds and considerations that figure into this process, and the way in which they enter. For expository expedience, we may distinguish three kinds of moves: (1) identifying the puzzle; (2) looking more widely around to the surrounding customs, practices, and circumstances; and (3) choosing sets of practices and circumstances and describing them as "game variations," showing the analogous and disanalogous rules, showing one game to be a case of another (apparent differences resulting from different circumstances), and the like.

Leach's arguments are directed against Spiro's line of approach, which fixes the breakdown in the same-practices rule at practices of natural explanation of pregnancy, and against the puzzle about their adherence to this false explanation that this line of approach commits him to. What sort of commitment is this? It is, in the first place, a revisable one. It may be, for example, that our attempts to explain their adherence to the false natural explanation turn up material that the initial translation cannot readily or plausibly be made consistent with. Or we may find that puzzle to be so intractable that we call the adequacy of the translation into question and revise it with an eye to these difficulties. Leach's criticisms point out implausibilities in Spiro's explanation that constitute grounds for such a revision. His move is to replace the puzzle to which Spiro's "ignorance" explanation is addressed. He replaces it by identifying the breakdown in the same-practices rule differently – as a matter of religious practice. The explanatory suggestions Leach goes on to make contribute nothing to answering the question "How could they adhere to this mistaken explanation?" – Spiro's question. It is Spiro's *formulation* of the puzzle as well as his explanation that Leach rejects. Leach answers the question about the Tully River religious dogma by offering an analogy, a description of the dogma as a variation of a familiar one.

In short, the explanation takes this form:

Just as Catholics believe that Jesus was born without human male sexual contribution, so do the Tully River Blacks believe, with this difference: they hold that all births occur in this way, where Catholics do not.

What does this account for, and how? To use a mechanical analogy, what he is doing is like taking a part from one machine and modifying it to fit another machine. The test of adequacy is that the machine does everything it did before. In the case of comparative sociological explanation, the "part" is a practice, from a culture or context other than the one in question, which is fitted into place by adding necessary variations (like generalizing the virgin birth myth from Jesus to all persons). The process of setting comparative sociological puzzles bears a resemblance to the identification of mechanical difficulties. (This analogy cannot be pushed too far; it does *not* mean that "connections of usage" are like mechanical links.) The Catholic dogma is a mystery, and what makes a mystery a mystery is that it is not explicable, because it is not a justified belief.[1] When Leach describes the Tully River doctrine as a variation of this, he is saying that it too is a mystery, and that it is not supported by justifications, as, for example, practical beliefs about animal husbandry usually are. If the Tully River natives had a justification – in the form of a theory of pregnancy based on practical experience, witchcraft beliefs, broader religious principles, or whatever – it would weigh against Leach's account. The Tully River beliefs would then not be mysteries, and the analogy would break down at the point of the connections to these other doctrines. Where the Tully River doctrines would have the connection, the Catholic one would not.

What we are concerned with in the case of mysteries, then, is not justification but other aspects of use: who affirms it and under what circumstances and motivations, how others respond to the affirmation, and consequences of various kinds for such things as theology, legal doctrine and practice, ways of coping with emotions and events, or whatever else turns out to be at stake. The question "Who affirms the belief and under what circumstances?" is an important part of Leach's case against the "ignorance of physiological paternity" interpretation of another famous case, that of the Trobrianders. He recounts R. F. Fortune's report in *Sorcerers of Dobu* of an attempt to stage a debate between Trobrianders, who denied the role of the father, and Dobuans, who maintained it. Fortune says that "the head of every Dobuan in the room immediately was turned away from me towards the wall. They affected not to hear the conversation; but afterwards when they had me alone they were furious with me" (quoted in Leach, 1969:121). The Dobuans would not, presumably, have reacted in this way to a discussion of what they took to be positions about facts of nature. As Leach puts it, "The argument was plainly about doctrine not about knowledge."

One especially interesting aspect of use, or "connection," that Leach points out in the Tully River case is the one Spiro's attack was directed toward, the use of the dogma in affirming that "the relationship between the woman's child and the clansmen of the woman's husband stems from public recognition of the bonds of marriage, rather than from the facts of cohabitation" (Leach, 1969:87). The way in which the Tully River dogma "says" this, or "affirms" it, is analogous to the way in which the Catholic dogma supports the claim of the divine paternity of Jesus. A virgin bears a child, the dogma holds, and who but God could perform such an act of fatherhood? In a ritual context like this, the divine paternity claim is a clear implication. In the Tully River case, the denial of human paternity carries the same implication, but it is applied instead to all births, and so its consequences are different. It precludes the possibility of "the facts of cohabitation" having any implications for kinship. This constitutes a backhanded affirmation of the fact of "public recognition of the bonds of marriage" as the sole determinant of the child's place in the kinship system.

The relation of the Tully River doctrine to other institutions, such as legal institutions governing inheritance, is not of much interest to Leach. Under both the ignorance interpretation and Leach's interpretation, it would be impossible to have a lawsuit brought by illegitimate children against a man's estate; for there could be no such thing as a man's illegitimate children under either interpretation.

For these connections, Leach's account explains the facts of use that Spiro's rule holds true for. There are other facts, however, which might bear differentially on the adequacy of the two hypotheses. It would, for example, be of interest to know something about Tully River birth-control practices. Are there any practices that reflect recognition of physiological paternity? Or is the no-contribution doctrine used to inform birth-control practices, so that, for example, attempts are made to avoid the heralds of conception that Roth lists? These questions are not examined in Roth's account. But they are a point from which subsequent investigation might usefully depart. This gives some suggestion of how our investigations are directed by previous explanations and of the disputes to which they give rise.

Where does this discussion of the pattern of argumentation and explanation being considered leave some of the issues of Chapters 2 and 3? It leaves Hollis's worry about the "uncheckable" nature of translations of ritual beliefs far behind. The example showed that there are indeed grounds for deciding between translations other than the look-and-see checks Hollis discusses; and it shows that these grounds are of use in settling translation issues in situations where look-and-see checks are not possible or relevant (a range of situations Hollis wished to abandon as insoluble in principle). The account also enables us to put look-and-see checks in a better perspective. Such checks settle some questions about translation, but not others. If, for example, a claim that "Where we say x, they say y" is made for the utterance x "The cat is on the mat," and a counterclaim is made to the effect that x should be "The dog is on the mat," we can decide between the two by looking for dogs or cats when y is uttered. But if another translator claimed that y was a curse uttered at cats on mats, these checks would be of no avail. To decide such a dispute we must look at other aspects of y's use: whether, for example, to utter it is taboo under certain circumstances, so that its utterance would cause consternation or elicit remonstrances not to say it in front of guests. Checking, then, turns out to be a much broader activity than the looking and seeing that Hollis takes to be definitive of checking a translation, and look-and-see checks can be seen to be one kind of check on sameness of use among many kinds, appropriate to one kind of issue among many.

Earlier it was remarked that the relation between translation and explanation was sometimes intimate. We can now see that the logical relation between this sociological issue and the translation issue is more than intimate. The hypothesis to be tested is a conjunction of the two hypotheses, that is, the two hypotheses taken together. One cannot test the one hypothesis without assuming the adequacy of the other. But because one does not ever test the two types of hypotheses separately, this "assumption" is more reasonably regarded as part of the hypothesis itself. Thus each translation has a "sociological" component, of practices that are assumed to be followed.[2] The fact that we test translations, or at least intelligibly argue for and against them, means that the sociological component is tested as well. So we have a criterion for evaluating the validity of the sociological component in the same sense that we have criteria for evaluating the translation. The criterion is exactly the same, because it applies to the conjunction and not to the translation or the sociological component separately. There is a recognizable sense in which the sociological component is a comparative explanation. So here we are dealing with a sociological explanation that we assess as we assess a translation, and in this sense we are treating sociological explanation as translation.

We can now also unravel some difficulties with Evans-Pritchard's discussion of Zande magic by seeing his analysis and the criticism Winch levels against it through this pattern of explanation in which puzzles are set and "game variations" are chosen, described, and elaborated.

Winch objects, it will be recalled, to two moves Evans-Pritchard makes: his negative comparison of Zande "magical" ways of reasoning to the ways of reasoning of Western experimental science, and his claim that Zande beliefs and practices do not conform to "objective reality." In short, it may be said that comparisons between the practice of Zande magic and of Western science may serve valid purposes and that the question of the relation to objective reality is a matter separate from the sociologist's explanations; these two points will be elaborated in order.

The tribes with which ethnographers deal commonly do not make the distinction among "scientific," "religious," and "superstitious" discourse that Western intellectuals have come to make in the last few centuries; so it is not surprising that sets of practices of these tribes may have characteristics of scientific thought, religious thought, and superstitions together with one another. In such cases, simple comparisons to our scientific thought, our religious practices, or our superstitions will not suffice. We may, for example, require comparisons to practices of ours that we regard as scientific, as well as to practices of ours that we regard as superstitious. In making such comparisons, it may be necessary to show how far each one may be carried. Zande thought obviously presents us with this sort of problem. What Evans-Pritchard shows us is how far the comparison to scientific thought may be pushed and where it breaks down, and in doing this he shows the futility of seeing the Zande system simply as another mistaken scientific doctrine, like the phlogiston theory or geocentrism. And this is worth knowing if we are to come up with an adequate explanation.

If we were to show, in the analysis of a particular body of tribal practice, that the religious analogy carried us so far and no farther, and the scientific analogy carried us so far and no farther, we would set up a puzzle that might be best solved by a comparison to both religious and scientific intellectual practices, noting the variation that the tribesmen do not distinguish between the two types of practices, scientific and religious, in the way that Western intellectuals have come to, but instead relate the practices in such and such a way. What would be of issue in a case like this would be differences in the rules for dividing up the kinds of activities.

Such cases arise, and in the face of them it would be simple dogmatism to insist, as Winch does, that the only appropriate comparisons for "ritual" beliefs and practices are to beliefs and practices that we call in Western society "religious." As Robin Horton has pointed out in his famous article "African Thought and Western Science" (1967), primitive people's ways of accounting for their universe may have certain very strong resemblances to Western ways of scientific reasoning, which suggests that advanced scientific theory may well provide a better source of material for game comparisons than Western religious doctrine. Which comparisons are most apt for a particular case, or how, in a particular case, the native ways of relating practices may be seen as variations of the ways we relate them (i.e., by distinguishing analogous practices into types like "scientific" and "metaphysical"), are questions for social inquiry, to be argued after the manner of the Spiro–Leach example.

Unfortunately, it has all too often happened in the study of the intellectual life of nonliterate peoples that very insightful efforts at bringing out differences between their ways and Western ways of reasoning about the world (in the jargon of this chapter, puzzle-setting activities) have often been followed by weak attempts at explanation. It goes without saying that labeling a set of practices "mystical" or "prelogical" is sham explanation, or at best like leaving a marker saying, "IOU an explanation at this point." Functionalist explanations typically are not much better. If we say, for example, that a particular practice promotes social cohesion, or that a particular ritual decreases anxiety (setting aside the monumental questions of the nature of the evidence that such explanations require), we have really said very little to answer the question "Why this particular practice?" After all, a *great many* practices that the group does not follow and that are recognizably different from their practices might also serve to promote social cohesion or decrease anxiety, and such explanations fail to distinguish between these.

Yet there is a sense in which the game-variation pattern of explanation described here is akin to functionalism. When a question over a practice has arisen in a comparison between two societies, sometimes part of the explanation of the practice involves pointing to aggregate ends (like social cohesion) or individual ends (like biological or psychological "needs") that two apparently different practices from two societies both serve; just as we might explain the difference in the rules of two canasta games by showing that both rules secure the same purpose, such as making it possible to accumulate sufficient points in the space of a few draws to turn a game around, thereby insuring that players who are behind will not lose interest in the play. Such explanations are only part of a game-variation explanation and need not always figure in the particular puzzle one is concerned with. However, it would be grounds for rejecting a solution if it has aggregate implications at variance with the aggregate facts, regardless of whether these facts figured in the formation of the original "puzzle."

Functionalism seems to result from succumbing to a temptation that such explanations can give rise to. The functionalist espies the ends to which the sociological explanation appeals, such as social cohesion, and takes the notion out of the comparative puzzle in which it makes sense and turns it into a general category. He is then tempted to conclude that these ends constitute some fixed set of "needs" that can be appealed to in any society. He thus makes an illicit transition between "We can explain some social practices by reference to their ends" and "There is a set of ends of social life and they explain social practices." It is not hard to see how the next steps – defining these ends and attempting to say what properties societies must, in general, have, in order for these ends to be satisfied – could become a major sociological industry; and this is the peculiar work that functionalist social theory made for itself.

The Spiro-Leach example illustrated some of the major difficulties formulated in the last chapter. A less arcane example of comparative explanation, which is relevant to more typical problems of sociological practice, is Edward Banfield's account of *The Moral Basis of a Backward Society* (1958), a study undertaken during the fifties of the small village of "Montegrano" in the south of Italy. The general problem that motivates Banfield is the question of the relation of the lack of concerted political action and corporate organization to economic backwardness. This is a problem with close links to one of the central problems of the sociological tradition, the question of the nature of the social developments that culminated in contemporary industrial Western society.

In discussions of economic development it is sometimes taken for granted that when certain technical conditions are met and certain amounts of natural resources are available, the organizational forms necessary for the utilization of the technology and the resources will arise relatively quickly, and the participants will soon acquire the organizational skills necessary to maintain the organizations. There are plausible alternatives to this hopeful view, however. One alternative suggests that the lack of organization and organizational skills itself precludes the creation of the modern economy and democratic political order to which the "developing" nations (or, at least, their Western-oriented elites) aspire. There is only one non-Western culture, Japan's, which seems to have the ability to organize and maintain the appropriate kind of political and economic associations. This leads one to suspect that the deficiency is, at the root, a cultural one.

It is this general problem that gives the case of Montegrano its interest: Here both the condition of economic backwardness and organizational deficiencies are present. But the case is not used to test a generalization about the relations of these two factors in economic development. Banfield is careful not to suggest that Montegrano is representative of the underdeveloped world, or even of southern Italy. Its value lies in the fact that here the general issue is manifested in a manageable form: The culture of the Montegranesi is different from our own, but not so different that it is impossible to pin down the cultural differences that are relevant to the problem, as it may be in societies whose cultural background is radically unlike our own.

He proceeds from a collection of impressions of differences between village life in Montegrano and small-town life in the United States.

In a typical U.S. small town, there is "a buzz of activity having as its purpose, at least in part, the advancement of community welfare," such as activities of organizations like the Red Cross, Future Farmers of America, Chamber of Commerce, and Parent–Teacher Associations. In Montegrano there is no newspaper; the only association is a "circle" of twenty-five men who play cards but have never undertaken a community project. There is an orphanage for children who come from local families, which needs food and repairs, but "no peasant or landed proprietor has ever given a young pig to the orphanage," and "none of the many half-employed stone masons has ever given a day's work to its repair" (1958:17). When asked, most people say that no one in Montegrano is public-spirited, and some find the idea of "public-spiritedness" unintelligible.

There are issues that seem to be ripe for political action. Many of the peasants are desperately anxious for their children to get ahead and recognize that this depends on educational opportunities. Although by law every child is assured schooling through age fourteen, in Montegrano only five grades are taught. The nearest middle school is not far, but bus schedules prevent commuting. The cost of sending a child to boarding school is prohibitive for peasant and gentry alike. Yet no action is taken to change the situation. There is no agitation to change the bus schedules or upgrade the local schools, and no candidate for mayor campaigns on the "school issue." The nearest hospital is five hours away by automobile, and the villagers have complained for years about it. Yet no one campaigns on the issue.

In Montegrano "an official is hardly elected before the voters turn violently against him" (1958:28). His supporters say – often truly – that he has become arrogant, self-serving, and corrupt. There is no party loyalty. The proportions of the local vote the different parties receive vary substantially from election to election. It is not uncommon even for officers in parties to change allegiances. For example, the secretary of the Monarchist Party changed his allegiance to the Communist Party and back again to the Monarchist in the space of a few months.

All this adds up to what Banfield calls "political incapacity." The political incapacity of the villagers is the puzzle he directs his explanations toward. Is there a real difference in ways of political reasoning here, or has Banfield misapplied our ways of political reasoning in the Montegranesian context? Some criticism has suggested just this (e.g., Muraskin, 1974). The criticism says that in the situations where Banfield is puzzled by the political nonresponse of the Montegranesi, he should not be, for there would be no chance of a political association's securing the desired ends, and it would be unrealistic for them to bother. Where Banfield takes his respondents to be offering rationalizations, they are giving perfectly good reasons. Banfield's misapplications of the ways of reasoning of American political culture in the Montegrano situations leads him to see things that demand explanation, not the conduct of the Montegranesi. His failure is to recognize our reasoning in theirs, a species of failure already noted in this discussion.

To the "tough-minded" empirical sociologist all this talk of "recognizing" and "discerning" must seem hopelessly vague, so it is worth spending some ink on the place of issues of the"misapplication" variety in sociological research. The sociologist commonly takes questions relating to aggregate patterns of conduct or consequences of conduct: spatial distribution in a city of activities like manufacturing, rape, or suicide or of events that are consequences of actions, like myocardial infarction; the distribution of such activities or consequences of actions, like wealth or prestige within a population; patterns that result from political acts like voting; and so forth. Much of the statistical analysis that is done in sociology is directed toward sorting out these patterns – decomposing them – in such a way as to identify differences in practices.

This statistical decomposing or sorting out is itself a species of explanation, and because sociologists do so much of this analysis it is easily mistaken for our quarry in this essay, the central conceptual features of distinctively *sociological* explanation. The distinction between the two may be made with the help of an analogy. Return to the population of DC-3s mentioned in Chapter 3, and consider a subpopulation of this, composed of the DC-3s owned by Fly-by-Night Airways. Aggregate repair reports show that Fly-by-Night's planes have a higher proportion of replacements of propeller bearings every year than does the total DC-3 population. When we explain this by saying that the DC-3s in the Fly-by-Night fleet are, on the average, older than those of the general population, we are not offering an *engineering* explanation of the difference. We are simply rearranging the data, decomposing the aggregate pattern, in such a way that an engineering explanation like "The older the DC-3, the more likely the propeller bearings will need replacement" can be applied. The rearrangement of the data is, however, distinct from the explaining of the causes of propeller-bearing wear. In the same way, the rearranging of data that goes on when we try to determine whether and where the same-practices rule has broken down is distinct from the explanation of the differences in the aggregate patterns.

What is the conceptual status of "aggregate patterns" in the context of setting puzzles about practices? Is there any question of insisting that the concepts used in describing them belong to the activities being studied? Think of a comparison between injury patterns in games played under various Little League baseball umpiring practices or baserunning rules. The concepts that go into the description of these patterns are obviously not dependent in any way on the concepts of umpiring and their application, but they certainly may serve us in indicating analogies and disanalogies in these practices. By the same token, aggregate patterns like those of urban ecology can be used to indicate differences in land-use practices without belonging to the activity of choosing places to locate homes and businesses.

This point suggests some other features of the activity of decomposing patterns and rearranging data in preparation for the explanations of differences between practices. One of the ways in which we recognize comparative puzzles is by tripping over differences in aggregate patterns. These differences may be the facts that set the comparative sociologist to work, rather than an immediate same-practices question about a specific practice. For example, in the United States, when the northern states are compared to the southern states, the proportions of party affiliates are found to differ. We may appropriately ask if this difference in aggregate patterns is a result of different practices in party allegiance between those who live in the two areas, or whether the same practices prevail and the differences result from the differing composition of the electorate. In order to answer the question, we may decompose and rearrange the data to reflect such things as differences in class composition, the rural–urban balance, and religion. Various well-known devices are open to us. We may arrange the data so that comparisons are made between aggregate patterns for subsets of the population with the same properties – for example, aggregate patterns for Catholics in the other society. Or we may generate two virtual or hypothetical populations, equalized mathematically on variables of interest, and compare the aggregate patterns of these virtual populations.

It should be clear that although differences in aggregate patterns may suggest that the same-practices rule has broken down, they do not assure that a breakdown has occurred. Similarities in aggregate patterns may conceal differences that would be apparent if the patterns were decomposed further, using previously overlooked distinctions; or the same aggregate patterns may turn out to be consistent with a wider range of divergent practices than one might suppose. The phenomenon of residential housing segregation by race provides a good example of the kind of difficulties that arise in making the transition back and forth from practices to patterns. The same patterns of extreme residential segregation between whites and blacks may result from all members of both races making their individual housing choices out of a desire for racial balance and on a basis that we would class as quite tolerant (such as willingness to live in any neighborhood in which their own race was

in a simple majority), or they may result from all members of both
races being intolerant and making their housing choices out of a desire
for segregation. (In fact, there are few combinations of desires that
lead, given free choice, sufficient time, and a stable size and mix of population, to anything *but* extreme residential segregation.) A sociologist
who concluded from the existence of major differences in aggregate
patterns of housing segregation between two societies that there were
substantial differences in choice practices, or concluded from the similarity of patterns that there were no substantial differences in practices,
might have been badly misled (Schelling, 1969).

Banfield might approach his problem through the assessment of differences in aggregate patterns. He might compute proportions of
villagers who belonged to voluntary organizations, or measure in some
way their contributions to associations formed for the public good, and
then compare these statistics and distributions with those for other
communities, in order to show significant differences, perhaps attempting to control for poverty, literacy, differences in proportions of members of various class or occupational groups, or whatever. Consider what
this approach might yield. It might show that persons who are partially
employed in more than one occupation typically do not participate in
political and corporate associations, and a high proportion of Montegranesi fall into this class; the pool of potential participants in Montegrano is therefore much smaller than it is in the towns to which
Montegrano is being compared, and the fact that such associations do
not exist in Montegrano is no surprise. Or it might be shown that participants in the kinds of associations Banfield finds lacking in Montegrano
are members of the middle class, so that there is still a puzzle, but it is
a puzzle over the conduct of the middle class and not over that of the
peasants and laborers.

But notice that if there are no purposes that would be served by
political association and if the villagers are reasoning about the potential value of these associations, just as small-town Americans would,
there is no comparative puzzle about the failure of the villagers to enter
into them. To make this decision these ways of reasoning must be correctly applied to the villagers' situation, and if they are misapplied, a
puzzle may appear as an artifact of the misapplication. Examination of
these aggregate patterns of participation cannot provide the needed
check on such a misapplication, for the aggregate pattern of low participation in political associations is consistent both with the practice of

ways of political reasoning that would lead to political association in situations where political association would serve no purpose and with the practice of antiassociationist ways of political reasoning in situations where political associations *would* serve a purpose. The examination of aggregate patterns, in other words, can only be a preliminary to determining if there is a breakdown in the same-practices rules, to recognizing our practices in theirs, or to identifying a misapplication of a compared practice in a different context. It cannot be a substitute.

The approach Banfield chooses to take to the practices of the villagers is more direct. He has the villagers display their ways of judging and reasoning about situations through projective tests, through answering questions about hypothetical cases, and through describing examples in which differences in practices and ways of reasoning may be identified. He does not ignore such matters as the effects of the poverty and illiteracy, which might be controlled for in a statistical approach decomposing aggregate patterns; he handles these matters in a different way. He calls them "underlying conditions" and treats them, along with other aspects of the villagers' situation, as constraints on the possibilities of action. This treatment is appropriate to his approach, for it provides a measure of protection against mistaking the examples of villagers' choices of action or inaction for examples of choices among a wider range of possibilities than is actually open to them.

Other questions that might be examined in a strategy of statistically decomposing aggregate patterns can also be dealt with in terms of Banfield's more direct approach. He does not systematically contrast the examples of conduct and reasoning of members of a specific class or occupational group in Montegrano to examples drawn from the conduct of members of comparable groups in small-town America; but he might, if questions about the effects of class or occupational structure arose, and remain entirely within the strategy of dealing with examples and constraints on choices. The question of the effect of the size of the pool of potential political participants could be handled through judicious comparisons as well. We can ask what small-town Americans do; what course do they take, if their numbers are equally small?

The conduct of southern Italians has long attracted explanations, and Banfield begins his own attempts to formulate an explanation by considering these. Poverty is often cited as the cause of their apparent peculiarities of conduct. The poverty is real. Many have only bread to eat, and little of that. The well-to-do of the town are poor by U.S.

standards. In such poverty, newspapers and the events they report could not be supported. Ignorance is another related reason: Illiteracy is high, and some peasants never have traveled beyond the next village. Such ignorance prevents the peasant from making meaningful political choices and even from having any notion of the possibilities. Class conflict is another explanation: The upper class offers no leadership because it lives by exploiting the peasants and can exploit successfully only by keeping them ignorant and in such poverty as to be economically defenseless. Another explanation points to the "despairing fatalism" of the southern Italian – his belief that his own action can do little to alter the course of events and that it is best to accept them resignedly and patiently as they come.

Banfield says that there is some truth in each of these theories, but none is fully consistent with the facts of conduct, and they will not tell us how a Montegranesi will act in a concrete situation. The poverty is severe, but it does not explain the fact that, although there is hardly a man in underemployed Montegrano who could not contribute a third of his time to some community project without a loss of income, no contributions of time are made at all. The peasants are not as politically ignorant as the explanation makes them out to be. The interviews Banfield conducted showed that the peasants could, for example, give a reasonably clear account of the claims and aims of the Communist Party. If we compare Montegrano's poverty to that of various small towns on the U.S. frontier with even more severe ignorance, poverty, and paucities of natural resources, we do not find the same apparent incapacity for self-government and mutual aid.

Class antagonism is no doubt an important element of Montegrano life. Banfield discusses at length the degraded status of the peasants and the low esteem in which their work and "country manners" are held by the gentry. Social intercourse between peasants and members of the gentry display the differences in their status sharply. Banfield says that "a gentleman who needs a donkey expects a peasant friend to supply one without charge," and that when a gentleman "buys a melon or a basket of tomatoes, he hands it wordlessly to the nearest peasant boy, woman, or man with whom he is acquainted who carries it home as a matter of course." The peasant does these things out of a desire to keep on the good side of members of the gentry, for "he knows that a time will come when the gentleman can give or withhold a favor or an injury" (1958:76-7). The patterns here are not feudal: There is no sense of paternalistic concern on the part of the gentry. The peasants, for their part, resent the real and symbolic aspects of these relations, and they are sensitive to insults (1958:82). (But by Italian standards, Banfield says, class relations are amicable.) He suggests that, as an explanation, class antagonism will not suffice. It founders against this question: Why don't the peasants unite against the upper class?[3] One might make the comparison to small-town economic antagonisms of the nineteenth century in the United States, which gave rise to all manner of united political action.

Similarly, though "despairing fatalism" may be a good characterization of the southern Italian's view of life, it will not do as an explanation. There are simply too many instances where he is not incapacitated by despair. Many peasants, for example, have begun to practice birth control in order to improve the lot of their children, an action that despairing fatalism would seem to preclude.

Banfield offers an alternative, which he says will

> make intelligible all of the behavior about which questions have been raised and will enable an observer to predict how the Montegranesi will act in concrete circumstances. The hypothesis is that the Montegranesi act as if they were following this rule: Maximize the material, short-run advantage of the nuclear family; assume that all others will do likewise.
>
> One whose behavior is consistent with this rule will be called an "amoral familist." The term is awkward and somewhat imprecise (one who follows the rule is without morality only in relation to persons outside the family – in relation to family members, he applies standards of right and wrong; one who has no family is of course an "amoral individualist"), but no other term seems better. [1958:85]

One might ask whether this sense of rule is consistent with the sense that has been discussed. Behaving as if following a rule is, after all, not the same as following one, and rule following is what has been treated here. Actually, Banfield is being unnecessarily circumspect in this formulation.[4] As he subsequently makes clear, a person who failed to act in this way would be thought of as failing to meet his responsibilities to his family – not living up to a moral "must." This is clearly a "right or wrong," which brings it back to Winch's sense.

Banfield brings out this aspect of the rule in a discussion of the Montegranesian concept of *interesse*. The word in Italian means both "advantage" and "cause of excitement or attention," as "interest" does in English. The Montegranesi, however, use it only in the sense of "advantage." In the Montegrano view, he says, "a parent must do all he can to protect his family. He must preoccupy himself exclusively with its *interesse.* The *interesse* of the family is its material, short-run advantage . . . Any advantage that may be given to another is necessarily at the expense of one's own family" (1958:115); and the responsibility to protect the *interesse* of the family overrides any responsibilities of charity or justice.

The family whose *interesse* one must protect changes in the course of life. As a child, it is the family of one's parents, brothers, and sisters (less so of half brothers and half sisters). As an adult, it is the family of spouse and children. Responsibilities to parents and siblings virtually vanish at the point of marriage, and responsibility to children vanishes when they marry. To aunts, uncles, cousins, and other relatives, no responsibility is felt, and often there is considerable bad feeling. To members of one's own family, acts of spontaneous generosity, more so than with us, are common; but if a person went out of his way to help another who was not a member of his family, in the manner of a friend, it would be said of him, "Has he no family of his own?" (1958:109). Consequently, friendship, as we practice it, is largely unknown in Montegrano. One takes certain pains to be on good terms with neighbors. But one also takes pains not to let the neighbors get too close. One of Banfield's data sources was Thematic Apperception Tests, and the stories that the peasants told about pictures revealed much about their ways of moral reasoning. A common theme was neighbors doing harm out of envy. One consequence of such fears is that they serve to preclude the Montegranesi from developing the close attachments of friendship characteristic of social relations in the small U.S. communities Banfield uses as an object of comparison.

So what does Banfield's hypothesis amount to? The rule states a concept of "interest" that is a variation of the other concepts of interest each of us is familiar with, like "enlightened self-interest," "public-spiritedness," and "shortsighted individual greed." The statement of the rule uses the terms that we might use in formulating rules embodying these familiar concepts and a term, "nuclear family," that we might use in describing and distinguishing our own moral obligations to our kin. The variant concept, formulated in this way, is to do the work of the Montegranesi concepts of *interesse* and of family responsibilities. In this case, the "work" is the making of moral distinctions, and the claim of the explanation is that the rule cuts up the moral world (which is to say, actions and the possibilities of action) along the same lines and into the same categories as do the Montegranesi when they act and judge acts.

Banfield proceeds from his formulation of the hypothesis by listing a number of claims that he calls "logical implications" of the rule, which take this form. Each of these claims serves to contrast Montegrano society to societies like those of the United States and Western Europe. Taken together, they account for the puzzling "political incapacity" of the village that Banfield began with.

Among the implications are these. First, in a society of amoral familists, no one will further the interest of the group or community except as it is to his private advantage to do so. A merchant explains the fact that he has never joined a political party by saying, "It isn't convenient for me – I might lose business," and then goes on to observe that those who run for office do so in order to "look after themselves." A schoolteacher, member of a leading family, expresses the same views – that those who belong to parties "are men who seek their own welfare and well-being" – and goes on to say that politics are a way of losing friends (1958:85–7).

Second, "In a society of amoral familists, office-holders, feeling no identification with the purposes of the organization, will not work harder than is necessary" to gain private advantage, and professional people "generally will lack a sense of mission or calling" (1958:91). The schoolteachers of the village, for example, often come late to class or miss it entirely. An engineer from northern Italy was shocked by this and remarked that in the north a teacher may hold informal classes, take the children on nature walks, or go on picnics. In Montegrano the "teachers spend the summer loafing in the *piazza* and they do not speak to their pupils when they see them." The pharmacist feels under no obligation to stock the medicines the doctor prescribes; for his part, the doctor, though a humane man, feels under no obligation "to provide himself with the bare essentials of equipment for modern medical practices" (1958:91–2).

Notice that this makes bribery and favoritism inevitable when opportunities arise, which in turn leads to a well-founded general distrust of the intentions of public officials. When there is a strong national government that keeps a stern eye on local affairs, these evils can be alleviated. Accordingly, the weak, who are less likely to benefit from bribery and favoritism, are likely to prefer a strong government, like that of the fascists (whose period in power is recalled with considerable favor by many of the peasants).

The Montegranesi assess the intentions of others by, in effect, standing the rule on its head. They proceed from the assumption that everyone else is maximizing his short-range advantage, and construe the actions and claims a person makes as attempts to further his own interest. Accordingly, an act of charity or public-spiritedness, regardless of its genuineness, is never taken at face value. This makes for a general atmosphere thick with suspicion, for mistrust of this sort is not easily satisfied. "Leadership" in the sense with which we are familiar is consequently impossible. No one will take the initiative to organize unless there is something in it for him. No one would follow, out of distrust for his motives.

A third implication is that "the amoral familist will use his ballot to secure the greatest material gain in the short run. Although he may have decided views as to his long-run interest, his class interest, or the public interest, these will not affect his vote if the family's short-run material advantage is in any way involved" (1958:100). Banfield's prime informant, a peasant who is a monarchist by family tradition and conviction, votes for the Christian Democrats because under them he has received a few days' work on the roads each year. He explains that "when we vote, we vote for the party that we think has given us the most" (1958: 100-1). Party workers are motivated in much the same way as the voters. The secretary of the Monarchist Party who changed his allegiance to the Communist and back in the space of a few months did so because the Monarchist headquarters was slow with his pay. When they settled with him, he returned to his duties as though nothing had happened.

Once Banfield has the matters directly covered by the hypotheses in hand, some aspects of the context can be fitted into place. The fatalism of the Montegranesi, which had been cited by earlier writers as an explanation of the apparent peculiarities of their conduct, and which Banfield amply documents in his TAT study, becomes understandable. The TAT results show a deep apprehensiveness among the Montegranesi. A very common theme in the stories is the possibility of one's children becoming orphans. This is a fear with a factual kernel, for to become an orphan is typically to be reduced to begging. Relatives take little responsibility for children other than their own, and when they are taken in, they are treated badly. The community, unlike many other agrarian communities in impoverished areas of the world, takes no responsibility for orphans. The view taken by both relatives and the community is in accordance with the hypothesis of amoral familism: The protection of orphans is outside the scope of any villager's *interesse.* The Montegranesi are also extraordinarily apprehensive about crop failure. The relation between the apprehensive–fatalistic way of facing the world and the general pattern of amoral familism may be summed up as a complementary one. The apprehensiveness and fatalism give the villager apparent reasons for placing his own family's short-range interest above all other concerns. The fact that he cannot expect help from the community or his relatives if his crops fail or protection for his children if they are orphaned – because the rest of the community members are looking after their own *interesse* – gives him something to be apprehensive and fatalistic about.

Taken together, these results give us our answer to the puzzle of the missing political and community activities. In the land of the amoral familist, it is only reasonable (even by U.S. ways of reasoning about self-interest and political action) to be an amoral familist oneself. If we look at the possibilities of political action from the point of view of the villager, we see that to act otherwise would be to act pointlessly. If a villager tried to initiate joint political action toward some community goal, he could reasonably expect that the effort would arouse the suspicions of others and fail to arouse support. If another person initiated such action, the onlooker could reasonably expect that he was doing so because there was something in it for him. And the villager could expect that his loyalty, once gained, would be abused. One is reminded here of the dilemmas that arise in nuclear war simulation games and the difficulties in moving out of situations of mutual high risk. How else is this explanation akin to explaining a game by describing one game as a variation of another? Describing Montegrano concepts of interest and family obligations as variations is akin to describing the different objects of different games. Saying how the resources of the Montegranesi differ is akin to describing differences between the powers given to the players in different games. The conclusion is akin to saying, "In game *B*, certain strategies appropriate to game *A* will not work, or would fail to gain the object of the game."

So what does this elaborate discussion of examples show? It shows that
there is an identifiable pattern, recognizable as a species of sociological
explanation, which can be explained so that two sets of difficulties do
not arise: the difficulties with the law account of sociological explanation that Winch points out and the difficulties that have been revealed
by Winch's critics.

*What you are saying, though, is not all that different from Winch –
that the sociologist identifies rules. So why the fuss?* The differences
with the kind of activity Winch suggests may be seen by considering
the term "grasp." The sociologist, in Winch's picture, grasps the rules,
and grasps the nature of conduct as an embodiment of rules. The sociologist can then reflect on the rules, but he has to grasp them first. Winch
has in mind mastering techniques like doing sums, and the way in which
these are grasped serves as a kind of model for him. We might call this
a "within-society" perspective, for it takes as its starting point the kind
of knowledge that people within a particular form of social life have
(Winch uses the example of engineering and says that the sociologist's
position most closely resembles that of the apprentice engineer).

The perspective that has been shown in the examples in this chapter
is something quite different. It is a comparative, or "outsider's," perspective. The approach to the rules is correspondingly different. With
grasps there are no grounds for argument: You have grasped the rule or
you have not. In this comparative perspective there *are* grounds: for
rejecting, revising, and replacing identifications of rules. So although in
a sense there is an agreement between saying, "Within this pattern of
puzzle setting and solving the sociologist identifies rules," and saying
something like "The sociologist's business is to identify rules and grasp
them, and thereby grasp the conduct that embodies these rules," there
are important differences. The identification of rules and elucidation of
concepts are embedded in, and informed by, two rather different kinds
of activities. The approach is radically different as well. Winch wishes to
draw conclusions about the possibility of sociological explanation on
the basis of general considerations about the concept of human action.
Here the concern is to find the sense that sociological explanations
make when they make sense, and to begin to see (as in the case of functionalist explanations) what temptations are being succumbed to, and
how we are led astray when the explanations fail to make sense. Someone has remarked on the difference between Ryle's *The Concept of
Mind* and Wittgenstein's writings on that same topic by saying that

when one finishes reading Wittgenstein one finds it entirely understandable to feel compelled to offer mind–body theories such as those of Descartes and his successors, whereas with Ryle one is made to feel like an idiot for having done so. I hope the same differences will be found between this essay and Winch's.

Then are you just telling us that sociologists give analogies? No, but it would not be surprising if I were just saying something like that. R. Harré, for example, argues that scientific explanation in the natural sciences, is, characteristically, the offering of certain kinds of analogies (1970:34–62). But more is said: that in the pattern of explanation this chapter identifies, analogies of a certain kind, which resemble analogies between games, are used; and that they are used in certain limited ways, to solve the puzzles set when a same-practices rule breaks down.

How does one identify a "puzzle" and know what contexts to compare? Isn't it necessary to have some general framework that serves to identify the fundamental or important puzzles? What is logically peculiar about the second question is that it seems to rest on the idea that "what is important" is something that can be decided in advance of explanation or apart from it. It is illicit to prejudge the question of which facts about society are truly "fundamental," as, for example, Leo Strauss does by identifying them with the *politeia* of classical political philosophy, or as Parsons does with those norms that contribute to "system maintenance." Assessments of what is fundamental, if they are ever intelligible as factual claims, may be based on a factually valid explanation, and not vice versa.

The examples discussed in this chapter both began with puzzles that were "superficial": the absence of voluntary associations among the Montegranesi and the peculiar notion of reproductive physiology of the Tully River natives. Yet in the course of the explanation we were returned to traditionally important questions, in the one case to the problem of "interest" and in the other to the problem of kinship. These problems were not arrived at as a result of any *a priori* estimate of their importance. But it should not be surprising that genuine explanations should return us to traditionally significant concerns: These concerns after all acquired their reputation for importance as a result of their having previously demonstrated their explanatory significance.

A puzzle arises in a direct way from the breakdown of a same-practices hypothesis. If we find ourselves in a given social situation and act on our own concepts, and these lead to difficulties, such as people reacting in the wrong way, we know – at least when the usual means (which are also rule governed) of finding one's feet with someone don't suffice – that different practices are being followed. If we appear in a peasant village and receive a hostile, suspicious response to actions that would ordinarily produce a friendly response in our home social context, we need an explanation. If we form a game-variation hypothesis about this, we can test it by acting in the way indicated by the hypothesis. Suppose we hypothesize that the peasants take a handshake and uninvited eye contact to be an insult. We can act in accordance with this rule and see if their response changes. If it does in some contexts, but not in others, we have a new puzzle. Typically, one such puzzle gives rise to another, so that our efforts at accounting for one difference in practice lead to a broader account. Ordinarily, the puzzles sociologists are concerned with arise indirectly, in connection with such questions as "Why do members of a particular social class perform such and such actions?" As I have suggested in connection with the "culture of poverty," there may or may not be a difference in practices underlying the apparent differences in conduct.

There is no need for a rule to say which "contexts" to compare. The term "context" is misleadingly reified here. Contexts are not pre-given units of analysis. As I have suggested, what counts as a context depends on the puzzle and the proposed solutions. The same-practices rule may break down at any time. It is a matter of discovery that we are in a situation where the rules are different, that is, in a new context, and it is a matter of discovery what the boundary marks of the new context are. The context from which we take the practices that we modify to fit the new circumstances is a matter of expediency. A bad choice makes the explanation more difficult, but we can give up and try again. There are no *a priori* "appropriate" comparisons, but there is a mode of argument that shows some hypotheses to be inadequate and others to be more adequate; so there is no need for a rule governing appropriateness of comparisons.

Where does this pattern of explanation leave the problems of reasons and rules versus cause and law accounts of explanations of action? In Chapter 3, the issue was left open. The causal law alternative, it was said, exhausted its informativeness at the point of the explanation of conduct under variant institutional forms, a point where the sociologist's interests typically begin. The difficulties with the causal law account arose in connection with the problem of formulating a conditional that distinguishes the cases under which the law is true from the conditions under which it is false. It is necessary to draw such a distinguishing line in order to turn a formulation into a *general* (and hence explanatory) law. Yet the descriptions sociologists work with, like "father's career," turn out to be especially ill suited to this line-drawing task. This was shown by contrasting two typical sociological formulations to the case of classical mechanics. We can say that a set of dynamical laws are true for physical objects that fall between certain upper and lower size limits, and that the laws are false beyond these limits. In the sociological case, issues arise over the applicability of the descriptive terms, like "father," to instances that occur in social contexts where different kinship institutions are found, and we cannot say whether the generalization is true or false in these instances. The question "Is the formulation true or false of the fathers in this social context?" runs into "Just who is 'the father' here anyway?" which is a question about the appropriateness of the application of the concept of "father."

The pattern of explanation and argumentation that was described in this chapter picks up the sociologist's concern at just this point. The examples show that the "rule" account can be pushed out to deal with these difficulties, or, put another way, that rule and redescriptive explanations can be fitted into a pattern such that differences between concepts like "father" are also part of the pattern, as accounting for the differences between the concepts of "interest" and *interesse* are part of Banfield's explanation. The "fitting in" or "pushing out" of the rule-description account amounts to this: Explanations of institutions are construed as a certain kind of redescription of rules; and sociological explanations of individual acts that rely on these rule explanations are also redescriptions. For example, the act of a Tully River woman who caught a frog and brought it into camp, in accordance with the ritual practice, would be redescribed as an announcement of her pregnancy.

This does not mean, however, that the analysis of sociological explanation presented here is tied to a "redescription" analysis of action explanations. Indeed, one would prefer to say that the question of the form into which ordinary reasons explanations can be analyzed (if such "analysis" is even an intelligible project) is independent of the question of sociological explanation and its form. The difficulty in making such a case is that there is no small set of possible causalist analyses of action each of which can be shown to be without implications for the analysis of sociological explanation presented here. In general, however, contemporary philosophers who defend a causal analysis of action explanation that treats beliefs as components of the "cause" of an action (e.g., Davidson, 1974, 1976) do so on grounds that are not inconsistent with this view of sociological explanation. Davidson concedes the distinctiveness of the language of ordinary action explanations and its irreducibility to the language of causal explanation, that is, of physics or chemistry. He argues that in describing the mental elements of human conduct, the physical description and the "reasons and beliefs" description are two descriptions of the same facts, but the relations of one type of description to the other cannot systematically be formulated as regularities (1974:98-9). This argument, incidentally, is strongly reminiscent of Weber's defense of the autonomy of sociology (1949:74-5). Because action explanations at the reasons level refer to beliefs, there is no question of sidestepping the problem of identifying beliefs. One of my central concerns here has been to show that if one wishes to account for reasons and beliefs sociologically, one accounts in noncausalist ways. In short, a Davidsonian causalist analysis of *action* explanations does not entail a causal analysis of *sociological* explanation, and indeed my account may better fit the analysis presented by Davidson than a causal sociology would.

Another way of describing this fit between sociological explanation and action explanations is to say that the sociologist has a particular distinctive "explanatory interest" in action, an interest that has been explicated here in terms of puzzles arising from the falsity of a same-practices hypothesis. The sociologist's interest in action is thus distinct from such interests as the neurologist's and the economist's, which may be equally legitimate, but which arise in different ways and have different solutions. The "sociological perspective," it may be suggested, is the perspective constituted by the pursuit of this explanatory interest. It arises in the same way under either a causalist or noncausalist analysis of action explanations, insofar as both appeal to beliefs or practices.

How about such concepts as values, a traditional concern of sociologists? Values are shown as rules, as practices in the making of choices. The concept of beliefs fits in easily as well. We come to our beliefs by using acquired skills of observation and judgment (in short, by rule following), and we put our beliefs to work for us by using acquired skills in drawing conclusions. Beliefs figure into the kinds of sociological puzzles this chapter has examined because differences in belief may point to differences in these practices (or in others – practices that govern the flow of information and networks of communication, for example). And reference to these differences in beliefs may be necessary in explaining other aspects of the situation. And what is a "social norm," if it is not a complex of ways of taking and judging acts, and acting for certain reasons – which are rule-following activities all?

What about such concepts as "alienation" and "anomie," which may be said to characterize the concepts of the actors and the actors' relation to *their concepts?* The distinctive feature of the history of the concepts of both alienation and anomie is that they acquired a wide use apart from the theories from which they originally came. People could learn to apply the concept of alienation without subscribing to the Marxian notion of "species-being," or the concept of anomie without adhering to the Durkheimian notion of collective consciousness. Thus both terms were originally theoretical terms in these theories, but they ultimately became observational. Although the warrants for the application of the terms may not be especially clear or clarifiable, it is at least plausible to use them in asking for a sociological explanation of the differences between the anomie of St. Augustine and that of the contemporary middle-class person seeking a meaningful lifestyle.

The relevant question about explanation is whether the warrants for the application of the term are not in themselves sufficient to explain whatever the term is claimed to explain – whether, in other words, the term carries any additional explanatory weight. It is scarcely evident that either term does. If one plausibly characterized the beliefs, feelings, and dispositions of an alienated person, one would scarcely have less of an explanation of his actions if one neglected to note that this characterization warranted the application of the term "alienation." This use of the terms does not entail anything about the possibility of characterizing the actors' states of mind independently of their concepts or their concepts independently of their states of mind, as did the original theories.

The whole idea of "games" is being overused here. Social life really isn't like games. So doesn't what you say amount to offering yet another theory of society, and one that is just as limited as those, like functionalism, that you describe as missteps?

To say that what has been said here amounts to offering a theory of society mistakes it utterly. If you insist on calling it a "theory," it is a "theory of social explanation." And at that, it is at most a theory of a particular kind of social explanation.

Even so, it is fair to complain that the idea of games is being over-used. What was claimed was that the explanations this chapter discussed were close *kin* to the kind of explanation that is available to us when we compare games. The emphasis has naturally been on the similarities between games and the activities that sociologists study, though there are differences as well. The appropriate question is "Are any of the differences such that the use of the resemblances as an aid in explication is vitiated?" A list of apparent differences might include these: With a game, we can say what is part of the game, and what is not; games come to an end; in a game, the participants start out equal and there are fixed, written rules and a fixed object of the game that all acknowledge; games don't change their rules, societal rules do change. Some of these, however, are the result of conceiving "games" too narrowly, of thinking only of certain kinds of games, like competitive ones. If we think of the dealer's advantage in gambling games or the dictatorial position of the leader in Simon says, the objection that the positions of participants in social life are unequal loses its force. If we think of games like follow-the-leader, snipe hunts, and ring-around-the-rosy, other apparent differences vanish. There is no object to these games that resembles the point-scoring objects of football or basketball, or the checkmate of chess, nor do they come to an end (people just stop playing), but they are games nonetheless. Wittgenstein asks us to "imagine people amusing themselves in a field by playing with a ball so as to start various existing games, but playing many without finishing them and in between throwing the ball aimlessly into the air, chasing one another with the ball and bombarding one another for a joke and so on." Now, he says, someone can say, "The whole time they are playing a ball-game and following definite rules at every throw." But, he asks, "is there not also the case where we play and – make up the rules as we go along? And there is even one where we alter them – as we go along" (1958:para. 83). (And isn't this one of the kinds of change that societal rules go through?)

Perhaps the difference that is the most plausible candidate for the role of "vitiator" is this: When we talk about games, we can ordinarily say what acts are part of the game and what are not, whereas boundaries often cannot be drawn around other activities. In the context of the kinds of puzzles discussed in this chapter, however, the difference does not lead to difficulties. A practice puzzles us. To ask whether another practice that occurs with this practice is part of the same game is to ask what? Would the question mean "Need this other practice figure into the comparison in order to make the explanation work?" If it does mean this, then a question of this sort would be settled in the course of constructing and criticizing the explanation.

This account of sociological explanation makes it out that men are everywhere strictly bound by rules, and hardly have room to breathe, much less engage in the spontaneity that makes life worth living. Surely that is a wrong view, isn't it?

When all is said and done, what you have described here is not really explanation of action at all. Explanations, at least full ones, are stronger stuff, aren't they?

These questions form a pair, each pulling in the opposite direction. In response to the second, it must be acknowledged that "rule governed" is a very weak sense of explanation if you are thinking "determined by" à la classical mechanics when you hear "explained by." Yet if an appeal to a rule suffices to explain "why" in a variety of ordinary contexts in which actions need explaining (and it does), it might be that a certain kind of "why" question is being asked in these contexts. And it is not clear what one would be doing if one insisted that the answers to these "why" questions were "not really explanation," other than insisting on some ideal of explanation – whose appropriateness and relevance is merely assumed and never established. The same may be said of the explanations of rules that have been characterized in this chapter. They are explanations, just as is what the person familiar with both cricket and baseball says in describing baseball as a variation of cricket to a cricket player. If these do not square with some ideal of explanation, imported from other contexts, and there are no other reasons for denying them the status of "explanation," so much the worse for the ideal and its importation.

In response to the first question, it should be said that just as our action is not everywhere bounded by rules, our action is not every where bounded by, or open to, sociological explanation of the sort discussed in this chapter.

The senses in which an action is rule governed may be fairly trivial, as MacIntyre's example of smoking a cigarette shows. But it is the rule-governed sense that is of interest in this pattern of explanation; for this is where a puzzle may be framed (for example: "Why do hardshell Baptists, unlike most Americans, have a prohibition on such indulgences, and why do they feel guilt over them?" – which is to say "account for the prohibitory rule" and "account for the rule that sorts these as appropriate objects of guilt"). The utilization of the pattern neither detracts from nor enhances the spontaneity of action.

Another way of putting the whole matter raised by these two questions is to say that these sociological explanations have a limited place. Sociological explanations are *one* of the kinds of explanations we resort to when our ordinary explanations and understandings break down: when a Tully River native insists that the male does not contribute to conception, or a peasant of Montegrano is unconcerned about the needy orphans of the village, or a hardshell Baptist finds guilt (and perhaps a special thrill) in a cigarette. We show that it is such an explanation that needs to be resorted to by showing that there is a puzzle over different practices behind our inability to make our ordinary explanations apply. And we do this by showing that it is the commonly followed practice of the Tully River natives to make these claims, of the villagers to respond in this way, and of hardshell Baptists to treat these acts as objects of guilt. The sociologist's explanations in these cases are directed toward these puzzles.

We may connect this up to a recurrent theme in the history of sociology: its competition with psychiatric and biological explanations. These are other kinds of explanations that are there to resort to when ordinary "reasons and motives" explanations break down. The study of crime and criminals poses a characteristic instance of this competition: Ordinary reasons and motives explanations break down or are inadequate to explain the criminal act; so it has been a constant temptation to resort immediately to biological explanations (the turn-of-the-century study of crime, for example, was obsessed with head measurement and the biological inheritance of criminality) or to the use of notions like "mental illness." Sociologists have opposed this by saying that these explanations have been resorted to prematurely. To a significant extent the criminal has his reasons, but they are reasons we have failed to recognize because they are not our own (just as the Montegranesi peasants' reasons for ignoring the orphans are not our own). Accordingly, sociologists have concerned themselves with such things as the criminals' variant perceptions of acts and individuals (which is a typical rule-following matter), and how they develop these perceptions (that is to say, acquire the perceptual rules). These do provide something to resort to, but it is something short of "mental illness" or "genetic weakness." The study of racial differences is a similar case. In a recent article assessing applied sociology (Street and Weinstein, 1975: 65), the authors take as one of its "greatest achievements . . . that it has played the leading intellectual role in substituting a social–structural and culture view for a biological one as the dominant interpretation of differences between blacks and whites." This case also illustrates most poignantly both the differences between the natures of sociological and biological explanations as resorts and the difficulties of disentangling their implications in particular cases.

What about the problems of explaining social change? Look at some of the actual explanations of social change that go into Bloch's account of the various transformations of feudal institutions in his *French Rural History* (1966). In a discussion of the decline of the practice of collective grazing in the sixteenth century, he points out that in many places extensive and continuous parcels formed by patient accumulation began to replace the traditional strip fields. The proprietors of these parcels could, because of the shape of their fields, restrict grazing to their own beasts. They rejected the practice of collective grazing for reasons of pride: "Considerations of rank made the thought of submission to rules binding on lesser folk intolerable" (1966:205). The explanation is that persons who were in a position to act on such considerations did not exist previously and that the refusal to participate of those who for whom it had become possible made the practice successively less workable for the others. This is an explanation in terms of the *reasons* of the various participants for abandoning the practice. Sometimes he explains by citing royal decisions or developments in legal doctrine secured by scholarly argument. These are reasons explanation as well. Other explanations refer to the debasement of the currency, the labor market, and other "conditions" that change the decision matrix of the participants.

Concepts are shown to be modified, replaced, or applied in new ways to new circumstances. These new applications and conceptual coinages are typically explained by describing the intellectual efforts that led to their being made and accepted into common use, as in this explanation: "The lawyers of the twelfth and thirteenth centuries who set themselves to study Roman Law ransacked their venerable authorities, the source of all wisdom, for precedents bearing on the social institutions of their own day, and on serfdom in particular" (1966:105). Commonly, practices that were originally simple expendiencies, but were followed for many years, came to be regarded as obligatory. He explains these cases by describing the role of appeals to "the customs of the place" in medieval juridical practice and in common political reasoning.

These are typical explanations of particular social changes. None of them is mysterious as to form. When Bloch explains acts, such as the refusal of certain proprietors to allow the collective herd to graze on their land, he does so in terms of the concepts of the actors, namely, their considerations of rank. The relation of the sociologist's concerns to the explanation of these acts is the same as with the explanation of other acts. There may or may not be a sociological puzzle about them. The "considerations of rank" to which the explanation refers may be opaque to us, or if earlier peasants could have acted on these considerations and failed to do so, this failure would be opaque to us.[5] In either case, we would set about to identify the breakdown in the same-practices rule that has occurred, and to account for the difference between the considerations salient to each. Puzzles are identified in such comparisons between historical societies just as they are in comparisons between contemporary societies. One clear example of such a puzzle relates to the concept and institution of serfdom. Bloch's discussion fits the pattern of this chapter quite readily. He describes the category of serf as a variation of the categories of *colonus* and *servus* in Roman law and in the social life of the late Roman Empire (1966:89–101). He does this by showing contrasts between seignorial institutions and conditions and those of the Roman system of slave estates (1966:68–9).

What about questions of power and domination, and the power structure? Doesn't this pattern of explanation simply pass over very important questions? The explanation of the abandonment of collective grazing is an example of the explanation of power and dominance, as well. It focuses on a question of leverage. In medieval society, the pattern of landholding was such that everyone was constrained to participate in collective grazing. The constraints were, in part at least, economic. Anyone who declined to participate would have lost his own right to graze his animals on the land of others, and would thereby have incurred the risk of insufficient forage. He would also have lost the droppings of the herd as a source of manure. Further, the shape of the fields of medieval peasants made it inconvenient to keep the animals from straying. Once certain holdings became large enough, however, these constraints were no longer common to all peasants. Those with sufficiently large holdings could conveniently keep their animals within their plots, and their plots were large enough that the risk of insufficient forage would not be much reduced by participation in the herd. These constraints were economic ones, and the explanation of the leverage that the group of peasants with large holdings could exercise over the institution of the collective herd is that they were free from such constraints.

In this case, the explanation is of a familiar type: economic explanation that abstracts reasons like "It would incur no greater risk" from the considerations that go into what the peasants do, such as "Our plot is big enough not to worry about having enough grass; if the snow is bad, and we don't have enough, then neither will anybody else," and "If we keep the pig in the herd, it won't do us much good because the rich ones have all the good land for foraging to themselves, and our pig will get trampled in the scramble for the rest." The terms "leverage" and "constraint" here are used metaphorically. The explanation of what the peasants *did* does not require these metaphors. They are no more than an evocative, shorthand way of noting the fact of the differences between the reasons that the richer peasants had for abandoning the practice and the choices that were open to them and the reasons and choices of the poorer peasants, and of noting the fact that the richer peasants could act in ways that made significant changes in the range of choices open to the poorer peasants. It is such differences and facts, of course, that questions about "power" and "domination" are about. These particular differences did not exist in medieval society, and a shorthand way of noting that would be to say that the power structure differed. This has obvious similarities to things we could say about games. We might say that the structure of control in follow-the-leader is different from that in add-on, and different yet from that in poker. In neither the case of games nor the case of societies, however, need our use of these terms suggest that we need a *theory* of structure of control or of power structures. An argument that we do need such a theory would have to show that we cannot explain the things we want to explain without one.

The pattern of explanation we have here, then, does what a pattern of sociological explanation should do. The explanations that fall under it serve identifiable intellectual purposes: They solve puzzles that arise in a particular way. There are clear kinds of grounds for revising puzzles and solutions. They preserve what Winch calls the significance of acts *as acts.* Moreover, these explanations fit with other explanations that occur in the discussion of complex social phenomena, such as economic explanations and explanations of individual action in terms of notions like reason, intention, preference, and evaluation. The pattern is recognizably "sociological." And it is a type of explanation whose intellectual legitimacy is not subject to profound doubts.

5. Recognizing the solution

Now that this pattern of explanation has been identified, another question needs to be faced. Is its range restricted to what is usually called comparative sociology, comparisons between societies; or is it that all sociology is comparative sociology, and the range of the pattern extends to all sociology? In short, where does this pattern fit into the sociological enterprise? Ideally, the answer to this question would be something like this:

Valid sociological issues are essentially comparative in character. Once this is recognized, the solutions that have been offered to these issues, what in the past have been called "sociological explanations," may be seen to separate into two classes: a class of explanations that fall under this pattern and a class of explanations that may be comprehended as missteps out of this pattern, or as succumbing to temptations to push explanations in this pattern in the wrong way.

This answer would bring us to the goal with which we began: a picture of sociological explanation that enabled us to find our way in the thicket. There is, however, no neat and convincing way of making that answer stick.

A rough case along these lines can be made, however, and in view of the nature of the obstacles to making a satisfactory case for this answer, the rough case can be accepted as a sufficient substitute.

The obstacles are these. The boundaries of sociology as an academic discipline are indistinct and determined by historical accident as much as by any essential commonality in its intellectual concerns. Albion Small's sociology department at Chicago "included a division of 'Sanitary Science,' in which courses were given on 'House Sanitation' and 'Sanitary Aspects of Water, Food, and Clothing'" (Dorfman, 1972:92). More recent disciplinary acquisitions of problem areas are scarcely less outlandish. Consequently, any argument which presumes that a sharp line can be drawn distinguishing "valid sociological issues" is doomed to failure.

An even more troublesome obstacle is this: Much of the history as well as the present of sociology consists of attempts to create a science of social life (or of various aspects of it) that proceed by first adopting a particular model of scientific method or theorizing and then searching for claims that can be made about social life that fit this model. The fashions in models have shifted again and again in the last two centuries, as different surface features of various natural science theories were deemed most worthy of imitation; so we can readily see the folly of many earlier attempts. It is, for example, easy to dismiss Charles Fourier as a crank for thinking that Newton's achievement in physics was the discovery of a single universal principle, the principle of gravitation, and imitating him by proposing that social life was governed by the principle of passionate attraction; for we no longer think of such simple, all-embracing principles as the mark of science. But we find it more difficult to dismiss George Homans as a crank for doing much the same thing, because he emphasizes surface similarities between features of his formulations and features of natural science theories that more recent commentators, such as the Logical Positivists, have emphasized.

To some extent, the concerns to which these attempts have been addressed are artificial. They are creatures brought into being by the choice of a model. To this extent they can be dismissed. But to some extent, these same efforts are addressed to concerns about society that are not artificial and cannot be dismissed. Fourier, for example, was fond of saying that there were four great apples in history – Adam's, Paris's, Newton's, and Fourier's. Fourier's apple was one listed at a price of fourteen sous in a restaurant in Paris, at a time when "in his home town a hundred pieces of superior fruit could be bought for the same cost" (Manuel, 1965:197). The question it led him to ask was about the possibilities of alternative social arrangements that would prevent such disparities, a recognizably sociological question. The problem becomes "How do you distinguish the Fourier looking for a principle in social life that will resemble the principle of gravitation from the Fourier asking about the possibilities of alternative social arrangements for achieving particular ends?" The answer that the two efforts have distinctively different origins – that the apple problem grows out of the ordinary experience of recognizing the bad consequences of certain arrangements, whereas the search for the principle is imitative and grows out of a certain picture of science – turns out to have little value. The two efforts become thoroughly entangled in Fourier's own work, and even more so in the work of later writers, like Marx and

Comte, whose concern becomes the *replacement* of schemes like Fourier's with other schemes that have the entanglement built in from the start. What the strong case demands, then – a separation out of the artificial issues – is a practical impossibility.

The "rough case," consequently, would support an answer that would conceive the phrase "valid sociological issues" of the strong-case answer more narrowly than would be allowed by actual use.

What narrowing would be appropriate? A look at the next part of the strong-case answer – that the issues are essentially comparative in nature – reveals one constraint on the choice of a substitute: the risk of circularity. Because the choices of verbal formulas that could be used as substitutes do not appear very attractive, I will rough the point out by examples. The suspicion of circularity can be avoided by using examples whose sociological significance is beyond dispute.

The question of the Protestant ethic in Weber involves what is essentially a historical comparison. Durkheim's concerns with the division of labor, suicide, primitive classification, and institutions like *mana* are all essentially comparative. For example, what gave the problem of primitive classification systems its interest is that the systems differ from one another and from "scientific" classification. The point of his explanation is to account for these differences. Weber's other interests are comparative through and through. What gave bureaucracy its interest for Weber was its contrast to other forms of organization. His characterization of types of authority was an effort to bring the differences under account. Much of the rest of Weber's work is "comparative sociology" in the restricted sense of comparisons between nations. The great concern of the German historical school in economics (especially insofar as this school was a seedbed for sociological theory) was the problem of the origin of capitalism. This was a comparative question as well. The comparison was across epochs, and not across cultures, but the approach was the same. Sombart's explanation of the change fits the pattern identified in the last chapter nicely: The pre-capitalist period relied on the concept of a "just price," where in the capitalist period, the concept was that of "market price."

One widely held view of the intellectual origins of sociology gives the central place to the problem of the decline of the *ancien régime* and the aftermath of the French Revolution. The proto-sociological elements of the response to this problem in the writings of Saint-Simon and his followers and in the "conservative" theorists like Louis de Bonald are comparative. These elements cluster around the new view of feudalism and feudal institutions these writers present, and the contrasts to contemporary institutions the feudal institutions present – a comparative problem. It was this new view ("new" in that it replaced the view the Enlightenment had nurtured) that later sociologists were to assimilate and build upon. The Saint-Simonians showed that they learned the lessons of this comparative study well. When they denounced institutions of their own era, they often did so not by the rationalistic arguments of the *philosophes,* but by showing their disanalogies to the feudal institutions from which they developed – their corruption under the ascendant bourgeoisie. When they proposed to abolish institutions, they were careful to keep in mind the positive ends that these institutions had served, and to replace them with new institutions serving analogous ends.

The utopian strain in postrevolutionary social thought has paralleled, and served as an intellectual resource throughout, the development of sociology. This strain, when its attention has been turned to existing social institutions, has been comparative: The comparisons are between existing institutions and hypothetical alternatives. Fourier's apple was significant because he could easily conceive hypothetical alternative social arrangements that would avoid the evil. The technique of comparing to hypothetical alternatives is one we constantly encounter in contemporary sociology. The problem of inequality, for example, is framed using this technique. Ideal aggregate patterns of economic, political, or social equality are formulated, and societies are examined to see what practices serve to produce divergences from it.

The problem of the development of society in its widest historical perspective was the concern of such figures as Henry Sumner Maine, Herbert Spencer, Tönnies, and, of course, Durkheim, in *The Division of Labor in Society.* That the problem amounted to a comparative question for them is shown by the way each of them solved it: by looking for the pivotal divergent practices or set of practices from which modern society results. For Maine, the pivot was that obligations derive from status in the one case, contracts in the other. For Spencer, military techniques of discipline and control were replaced by industrial techniques of assuring voluntary cooperation. For Tönnies, personal relations motivated by sentiment were replaced by relations motivated by interest. Durkheim's categories of mechanical and organic served similar purposes: They distinguished ways of relating.

Contemporary sociological issues, no less than the great issues of the history of the discipline, have this comparative character. One way this can be shown is by considering the distinctions we make between psychological and sociological questions in areas like aging, art, science, deviance, and organizational life, where there are both "psychologies" and "sociologies." When a psychological explanation of conduct in those areas is offered, and we wish to dispute the explanation by claiming that the issue is (at least to an extent) a sociological one, we show that the individual variations that the psychological hypothesis accommodates, such as the hypothesis that there is an intrinsic decrease of ego energy in the latter part of life (Rosen and Neugarten, 1960:62), are not random across such things as social classes, cultures, or ethnic categories. In short, we show the question is a sociological one by showing that we can frame a comparative question. Most of the remaining areas that have become focuses of sociological interest are, so to say, intrinsically comparative. Marriage and the family, class, class arrangements, religion, occupations and professions, and urbanism all may be described in this way. The class of "valid sociological issues" for which the rough case can be made, then, is a large and fairly coherent entity, and is also nearly coextensive with the actual use of the phrase. The remainder of the ideal answer, that sociological explanations may then be seen to fall into two classes, a class of explanations in the pattern and a class of missteps out of the pattern, presents more serious difficulties. Here the magnitude of the obstacle created by the imitation of various models of natural science becomes clear.

In spite of this, a good deal can be said in the way of pointing out how explanations are missteps or how the urge to offer them is induced by pushing the pattern in the wrong way. Some of those missteps have already been described. In the last chapter, functionalist explanation, with its resultant ontology of "systems," "system needs," and the like, was seen as arising from comparative explanations like those which show that two apparently different practices from two social contexts serve the same ends. It was said that the functionalist made an illicit transition, a transition that resembles going from "All chains end somewhere" to "There is somewhere that all chains end." In Chapter 3, the substitution of explanations of action following the "attitude model" for ordinary "reasons and motives" explanations was discussed. It was suggested that sociologists were led to see the substitution as necessary by taking a too narrow view of the rules and reasons that operate in given situations, like the situations LaPiere created with his Chinese couple.

Nineteenth-century social theorists were capable of offering intelligent and improvable accounts of the particular social changes that went into the development of modern society out of traditional society. The temptation they succumbed to was to take what would be best understood as solutions to particular, limited, diachronic comparative puzzles and to generalize them into, or construe them as, theoretical *principles* of historical change. This temptation is easily understood when we consider it in the historical atmosphere of the success of Darwin's account of biological evolution and of Laplacian pronouncements. The consequences of the succumbing or the misconstrual, however, were serious. They led straight to various forms of what Popper was later to assail as "historicism." In subsequent years this misstep was not retraced but compounded. The obvious deficiencies of the proposed principles led not to a rethinking of the explanatory problem, but to the notion that "a general theory of social change" was a pressing need of sociology, a notion that, together with the functionalist notion of system needs and the influence of a variety of new choices of surface features of natural science theories, largely constituted "sociological theory" in the mid-twentieth century.

Another misstep occurs at the point of framing problems. In discussing the utopian tradition it was remarked that it was possible to describe the ideal aggregate patterns, such as a pattern of general economic equality, and to compare particular societies that diverge from this ideal in an attempt to identify the practices that account for the divergence. The use of a single ideal standard tempted the supposition that there was, rather than just a number of distinct problems of inequality, each with its own explanation, a *general* problem of inequality, calling for a *general* theoretical explanation (like Davis and Moore's functionalist theory of stratification).

The notorious "problem of order" seems to involve a related misstep. We can explain, in the framework of the limited pattern of comparative explanation of Chapter 4, particular means of attaining aggregate ends like "order" and particular occurrences of "disorder." But because "order" is an aggregate description with (at least the appearance of) general applicability, it is supposed that it constitutes a general problem, demanding a general explanation.

Durkheim, especially in *The Rules of Sociological Method,* recognized that aggregate patterns could often be assessed and described with greater precision and in ways that offered less invitation to charges of subjectivity than could customs and ways of reasoning. This led him to suggest that sociologists concentrate their attention on these patterns and the relations between them. Once he had, for these epistemological reasons, imposed this limit on his class of possible explanans and explananda, he made what could be called the DC-3 misstep. What he had were statistical relationships with the (genuine) explanatory force of the analyses an auditor would produce to show that Fly-by-Night Airways was not replacing too many propeller bearings. What, under the influence of the model of nineteenth-century physics, he was led to mistake these statistical relationships for were approximations of "laws of collective consciousness." The idea of the collective consciousness proved to be something of an embarrassment, and the model of science Durkheim adhered to lost some of its fashionability; so subsequently those sociologists who concerned themselves with statistical relationships grew less candid about what kinds of natural science formulations their formulations of these statistical relationships were supposed to resemble. What the standard manner of formulation conceals is that, as was noted in Chapter 3 in connection with the Duncan–Blau occupational-structure model, the relations hold by virtue of the fact that certain practices are followed, and that this is the fact that needs explanation (cf. Turner, 1977).

This is hardly an exhaustive list, but it points the way. Filling it out is a task for another time. It is enough of a list, however, to make the rough case. And this is an area of inquiry where rough cases are usually the best.

If we accept this case, where does it leave us with the problems with which the inquiry began? The proximate target of the inquiry was to establish an alternative arrangement of the material which avoided the difficulties of the law account that Winch's criticism made apparent and also avoided the difficulties that arose with Winch's version of the rule account. Both Winch's account and the law account identified a class of valid or nonelliptical explanations, both assimilated apparently unconnected or superficially different cases of explanation to this class, and both denied the validity or nonellipticality of another class of cases. Similarly, both accounts claimed to cover the range of cases of concern for the study of human action. Each account offered a model of the enterprise of understanding action that a sociologist seeking cues to guide his own efforts could follow. Winch's model stressed the mastery of rules, and grasping them from within the form of life in which they were followed. The law model may be constructed in a good many ways, according to the variety of cases it is stretched to cover, but the usual features of the model are familiar enough. Understanding of individual cases of action (or "behavior") is gained through the discovery of the regularities or stochastic laws, preferably quantitative in form, that the actions fall under. Each of these philosophical models has affinities to distinct styles of doing sociology. The Winch model has affinities to "interpretive" sociologies, although the relationship between the model and these sociologies must be characterized as subject to substantial qualifications. The law model has apparent affinities to "hard-data" sociologies, but this relationship, too, must be characterized as subject to important qualifications.

The alternative arrangement presented in the latter chapters was an effort of generally the same character as Winch's account and the law account. Like these accounts it distinguished certain valid and non-elliptical explanations, assimilated others, rejected others, and claimed to cover the cases. There were, however, some important differences. The problem that concerns Winch and that has typically concerned advocates of the law account is to make various general considerations about the nature of human action square with various general considerations about the nature of adequate explanation. Their conclusions about the nature of sociological explanation are incidental, though by no means without significant relevance, to their conclusions about this broader problem. The arrangement of material that was presented here started at the other end, so to speak. It started with those of the difficulties that have surfaced in the course of the controversy over the Winch thesis which are directly germane to the problem of sociological explanation. It was apparent that cases involving comparisons between societies were one kind of case that was a source of difficulty for both the law account and for Winch. The law account seemed to run into difficulties over what MacIntyre calls the "essential contestability" of some social concepts, concepts that, it seems, must figure into statements of many of the laws one would have to suppose necessary for a reasonably complete sociology. With Winch's account, it was not clear how we could offer a comparative explanation at all.

The presentation of the alternative arrangement of the material began with a consideration of two examples of comparative explanations. The concerns that motivated these explanations, it turned out, could be precisely specified by formulating them as comparative puzzles of a particular kind. In defining the puzzle, we proceed as though we hypothesized that *where we would follow such and such a rule, the members of another social group or persons in another social context would do the same.* This was called the same-practices hypothesis. The puzzle is set by identifying the breakdown in the hypothesis. The explanations that constitute the solutions to these puzzles, it was suggested, are kin to another, familiar, kind of explanation: the explanation of a game "by describing one as a variation of another – by describing them and *emphasizing* their differences and analogies." The different practice in a social group or social context that raises the puzzle is explained in the way that a different rule of a game is explained.

Very often the sociologist is concerned with explaining differences in aggregate patterns between social groups or categories. This interest was compared to the interest a physician might have in Little League baseball injury patterns under different rules. The relationship between rules and aggregate patterns goes both ways: A difference in aggregate patterns may indicate a difference in rules, and therefore may indicate the existence of a sociological puzzle. Methods of organizing data and statistical techniques may enable the sociologist to decompose the aggregate patterns either to show that the differences do not exist under the appropriate comparisons or to specify more precisely where the differences lie. Much of the statistical analysis sociologists do, accordingly, can be assimilated to the pattern of puzzle setting and solving that was identified in the two examples. The place of the statistical analysis, however, is limited: Analysis of aggregate patterns can help set up puzzles, and differences in aggregate patterns may require explanations that cite differences in practices. But the question "Why the different practice?" is not touched by the analysis.

The concerns of the interpretive sociologist may also be assimilated to this pattern, but not without an important alteration in our conception of these concerns. The traditional difficulties with the question of what evidence is appropriate to deciding between interpretations begin to look as though they result from a wrong view of the process of "interpretation." If the process is conceived in accordance with the "grasps" metaphor, it is senseless to even talk of "grounds" and "evidence" in connection with interpretations.[1] Yet evidence and grounds *are* offered when questions arise. Consider a fairly typical case:

Max Weber and Werner Sombart concentrated attention on the "spirit of capitalism" and on psychological and sociological analysis of the *Weltanschauung* of the early type of bourgeois capitalistic entrepreneur . . . The theories advanced by these two men launched a controversy which lasted until the early '30's, by which time they were largely discredited by the economic historians who had demonstrated the existence of commercial, industrial, and finance capitalism as early as the thirteenth century. [Ferguson, 1963:viii]

We can see quite readily how the economic historians' evidence is relevant if we discard the "grasps" metaphor and replace that picture with the puzzle-setting pattern. What the economic historians showed was that there was no puzzle about the contrast between the "mentalities" of the sixteenth-century economic actor and the mentalities of the economic actors of the immediately preceding centuries, for the practices did not significantly differ. And by showing this they deprived Weber's and Sombart's interpretive explanations of their explanatory object, just as Banfield's critics wished to deprive his explanation of its object.

This arrangement of the material led to a denial of the validity or adequacy of a variety of explanations. Among these were functionalist explanations and explanations that followed a simple "attitude–action" model. In the discussion of turning "tendency statements" into general, and hence explanatory, laws, difficulties were pointed out that have the effect of excluding as defective a very large class of formulations of the Blau–Duncan occupational-structure type. Anyone seeking a reason for the exclusion of explanations of the "law of social development" type was referred to Popper's well-known criticisms of the confusion of trends and laws.

The claim that the range of cases was covered was supported by showing that, once these and various other suspect explanations and concerns were eliminated, the concerns of sociologists could be seen as essentially comparative in character. It was acknowledged that there were difficulties in making the case that explanations which could not be assimilated to the puzzle-solving pattern were either defective or nonsociological. These difficulties were attributed to peculiarities of disciplinary history, and it was urged that they were fundamentally rhetorical and should not be taken as indications that the claim was mistaken.

The cues this arrangement of the material gave to the practicing sociologist and the "model of inquiry" that emerged in the course of the study differ significantly from the cues and models that were encountered in the earlier chapters. The questions that sociologists ask were pictured as limited puzzles, with origins in the ordinary experience of encountering social contexts where the practices of familiar contexts do not fit, or with origins in the discovery of differences in aggregate patterns that indicate differences in practices. This sort of puzzle was fitted into the concerns of psychology and biology with human action by suggesting that the need for sociological explanations of human action arose with a distinct kind of breakdown in our understanding of an act (or of an aggregate pattern).

The cues for the practicing sociologist came down to the suggestion that he reconstrue his own activities in accordance with the puzzle-solving pattern. The case for reconstruing them in this way is precisely that by doing so very real difficulties can be avoided – the difficulties with other explanatory forms that became evident in the course of the discussion. Moreover, they can be avoided without thereby sacrificing any of sociology's distinctive concerns. And by performing the reconstrual, the distinctive empirical concerns of "interpretive" and "statistical" sociologies, usually thought of as antithetical or mutually irrelevant, can be made to mesh. The tactics of both play identifiable parts in the process of setting and solving these comparative puzzles.

Notes

Chapter 1. Introduction: the object of sociological explanation

1 The relationship between the views of Winch and those of this group is discussed in McCarthy (1973) and in Wellmer (1970); Wellmer relies on remarks of Habermas in *Zur Logik ker Socialwissenschaften* (1970). In short, the relationship amounts to this: The hermeneutic group wishes to understand society after the fashion of Winch but then to go beyond this kind of understanding to a "theoretical understanding." Bar-Hillel (1973) has raised serious questions about the coherence of Habermas's arguments for the necessity for such "theoretical understanding." Also cf. Giddens (1976:44–70).

2 D. R. Bell says: "I have developed the startling parallels between Mead and Wittgenstein in an unpublished paper read at Leeds in 1960. Mead's views on the social nature of language are explicitly developed against both Watsonian behaviorism and traditional concept empiricism. He thus stalks Wittgensteinian game" (1967:122). Similarities are also remarked on in Miller (1974:66–7).

Chapter 2. Winch's account of the sociological explanation of action

1 Note that O does not have to agree with N's rule that a vote for Labour is a vote for industrial peace.

2 Of course, he might have a misguided idea; and if he did, the observer would want to make that clear in his explanation.

3 Particular cases could, of course, be explained away by imputations of bastardy.

4 This view has been popularized in the United States by Abel (1948).

Chapter 3. Some criticisms of the Winch thesis

1 LaPiere uses all these terms to define "social attitude."

2 This does not, of course, mean that Winch would deny that individuals may act paradoxically, inconsistently, or erratically, or that they may lie and speak insincerely. He would, however, deny that we could characterize their behavior in these ways unless we had a satisfactory understanding of the concepts that governed the context in which these acts were performed – because these characterizations are supported by setting the acts against the rules.

3 Hempel (1959) is a source familiar to sociologists. An excellent review of the problems may be found in Scheffler (1969:50–2).

4 The basic positivist statement on Sociology, Otto Neurath's early (1931–2) "Sociology and Physicalism," claims that "the sociologist is completely unimpeded in his search for laws. The only stipulation is that he must always speak, in his predictions, of structures which are given in space and time" (1959:301). The problem for the positivist is that a formulation which is limited in time and space is not explanatory, at least according to later attempts to

solve the problem of distinguishing accidental and nomic regularities. This intuitive demand is expressed in, for example, Hempel and Oppenheim's requirement that a general law be contained in the *explanans* (Scheffler, 1969:29; cf. Nagel, 1961:49–52, and Turner, 1977).

5 This is the case within certain limits. See Quine (1969) on the indeterminancy of translation.

6 Lévi-Strauss, in *The Savage Mind* (1966), adopts a thesis something like this.

Chapter 4. A pattern of explanation

1 It may be noticed here that although Leach and Spiro both tend to use such notions as "dogma" as though they were general categories of belief or utterance that can be applied universally, it is unnecessary to these translations and explanations that the concepts be taken in this way. In this context, one can simply speak of the analogy to the Catholic uses of "dogma" and "mystery," without any reference to a universal category of "dogma" or mystery."

2 Putnam makes this point and includes certain psychological assumptions as part of the translation process. In one example, he describes going to a gas station in Israel and saying *bedok et hashemen* for "check the oil." He remarks that if the attendant punches him in the nose, his "faith in the translation . . . will be shaken." He points out that in doubting the translation he makes such psychological assumptions as that "the attendant wants to sell gas and oil." It may be noted that one's faith in the translation is not dependent on this assumption in the same way as it is on "sociological" assumptions, because one's faith in the translation may be restored by encountering a less surly attendant. One can separate the psychological assumption from the translation by trying it on a new individual. A "sociological" assumption, such as an assumed obligation to be polite in response to such requests, ordinarily involves everyone in the context in which one tries out the utterance, and not one individual or another; so one cannot separate, for example, the failure of a translation of "hello" and an insulting fashion of opening a conversation, without forming and trying a new hypothesis (1978:69).

3 The fact that no attempts at organizing by the peasants against the upper class have been made may not be as significant as Banfield supposes.

Again, it is worth asking the critic's question: What would be the point of such organizing, in this case, by the peasants against the upper class? Banfield himself quotes a peasant who notes that land reform, one standard political goal, would be pointless in Montegrano, because the only person with enough land to divide up already has divided his land among tenants, and it is supporting as many families as it can be expected to (1958:36). Similar things could be said about the infeasibility of other political ends for which the peasants might unite against the gentry. This issue is a version of the question whether there is any difference in the political practices of the Montegranesi, and it can be addressed using the kind of argument we have become acquainted with as puzzle setting.

4 When Banfield states this "as if" formulation, he cites a famous article of Milton Friedman's, "The Methodology of Positive Economics" (1953), in which the "as if" device is used as a qualification attached to the assumptions about "rationality" economists use, in order to make clear the distinction between these assumptions and such things as empirical claims about human nature. The "as if" formulation is a difficult formulation *not* to go beyond, because usually one can: Friedman himself does, in this same essay, by pointing out that if a firm did not act "as if" it were following the principles economists study, it would go broke (a claim that is not without analogy to Banfield's conclusions about constraints on political action). The ambiguity between these uses is the subject of a substantial literature of its own (e.g., Nagel, 1963). Suffice it to say that Banfield goes far beyond the minimal "as if" use, in ways that are indicated in these pages, and can be most profitably read in terms of these further uses.

5 If we claimed that they could not have acted out of these considerations because no one's plot was large enough, we would be denying that there was any puzzle.

Chapter 5. Recognizing the solution

1 I vividly recall an exchange between an experimental social psychologist and a symbolic interactionist that went like this:

Experimentalist: In my work, we have statistical tests to tell us whether or not a hypothesis is correct. I've often wondered how a symbolic interactionist tells when he is correct.

Symbolic Interactionist (after some hemming and hawing): Well, a light sort of goes on in your head.

References

Abel, Theodore, 1948. "The Operation Called *Verstehen.*" *American Journal of Sociology* 54: 211-18.

Anscombe, G. E. M., 1957. *Intention.* Oxford: Basil Blackwell.

Baker, A. J., 1960. "The Philosophical 'Refutation' of Pareto." *Mind* 69:234-43.

Banfield, Edward, 1958. *The Moral Basis of a Backward Society.* Glencoe: Free Press.

Bar-Hillel, Y., 1973. "Habermas' Hermeneutic Philosophy of Language." *Synthese* 26:1-12.

Bell, D. R., 1967. "The Idea of a Social Science." *Proceedings of the Aristotelian Society.* Supplementary vol. 41:115-32.

Blau, P. M. and O. D. Duncan, 1967. *The American Occupational Structure.* New York: Wiley.

Bloch, Marc, 1966. *French Rural History.* Trans. by Janet Sondheimer. Berkeley and Los Angeles: University of California Press.

Bradley, M. C., 1960. Review of *The Idea of a Social Science. Mind,* n.s. 69:272-4.

Braithwaite, R. B., 1953. *Scientific Explanation.* Cambridge: Cambridge University Press.

Bryant, Christopher G. A., 1970. "In Defence of Sociology: A Reply to Some Contemporary Philosophical Criticisms." *British Journal of Sociology* 21:95-105.

Cavell, Stanley, 1969. *Must We Mean What We Say?* New York: Charles Scribner's Sons.

Chomsky, Noam, 1968. *Language and Mind.* New York: Harcourt, Brace and World.

Davidson, Donald, 1963. "Actions, Reasons, and Causes." *Journal of Philosophy* 60:685-700.

    1974. "Mental Events," in L. Foster and J. W. Swanson (eds.), *Experience and Theory.* Amherst: University of Massachusetts Press.

    1976. "Hempel on Explaining Action." *Erkenntnis* 10:239-53.

Dorfman, Joseph, 1972. *Thorstein Veblen and His America.* 7th ed. Clifton, N.J.: Augustus M. Kelly.

Ferguson, Wallace K., 1963. Introduction to Alfred von Martin, *Sociology of the Renaissance.* New York: Harper Torchbooks.

Frazer, James, 1941. *The Golden Bough.* 1 vol. abridged ed. New York: Macmillan.

Friedman, Milton, 1953. *Essays in Positive Economics.* Chicago: University of Chicago Press.

Frisby, David, 1972. "The Popper-Adorno Controversy: The Methodological Dispute in German Sociology. *Philosophy of Social Science* 2:105-19.

Giddens, Anthony, 1976. *New Rules of Sociological Method: A Positive Critique of Interpretative Sociologies.* New York: Basic Books.

Habermas, Jurgen, 1970. *Zur Logik de Socialwissenschaften.* Frankfurt: Suhrkamp.

Harré, Rom, 1970. *The Principles of Scientific Thinking.* Chicago: University of Chicago Press.

Hempel, C. G., 1959. "The Logic of Functional Analysis," in L. Gross (ed.), *Symposium on Sociological Theory.* Evanston, Ill.: Row, Peterson.

Hollis, Martin, 1968. "Reason and Ritual." *Philosophy* 43:231-47.

Horton, Robin, 1967. "African Thought and Western Science." *Africa,* nos. 1 and 2, pp. 50-71, 155-87.

Jarvie, I. C., 1972. *Concepts and Society.* London: Routledge and Kegan Paul.

LaPiere, Richard T., 1934. "Attitudes vs. Actions." *Social Forces* 13:230-7.

103

Leach, Edmund K., 1969. "Virgin Birth," in *Genesis as Myth and Other Essays*. London: Jonathan Cape.

Lévi-Strauss, Claude, 1966. *The Savage Mind*. Chicago: University of Chicago Press.

Louch, Alfred, 1963. "The Very Idea of Social Science." *Inquiry* 6:273–86.

————— 1966. *Explanation and Human Action*. Berkeley and Los Angeles: University of California Press.

Lukes, Stephen, 1967. "Some Problems about Rationality." *Archives Européenes de Sociologie* 8:247–64.

McCarthy, Thomas, 1973. "On Misunderstanding 'Understanding.'" *Theory and Decision* 3:351–70.

MacIntyre, Alasdair, 1967. "The Idea of a Social Science." *Proceedings of the Aristotelian Society*. Supplementary vol. 41:95–114.

————— 1971. "Is a Science of Comparative Politics Possible?" in *Against the Self-Images of the Age*. New York: Schocken.

————— 1973. "The Essential Contestability of Some Social Concepts." *Ethics* 84:1–10.

Manuel, Frank E., 1965. *The Prophets of Paris*. New York: Harper & Row.

Melden, A. I., 1961. *Free Action*. London: Routledge and Kegan Paul.

Mill, John Stuart, 1843. *On the Logic of the Moral Sciences (A System of Logic, Book VI)*. 1965. Indianapolis: Bobbs–Merrill.

Miller, David L., 1974. *George Herbert Mead: Self, Language, and the World*. Austin: University of Texas Press.

Muraskin, William, 1974. "The Moral Basis of a Backward Sociologist: Edward Banfield, the Italians, and the Italian Americans." *American Journal of Sociology* 79:1484–96.

Nagel, Ernest, 1961. *The Structure of Science*. New York: Harcourt, Brace, and World.

————— 1963. "Assumptions in Economic Theory." *American Economic Review*. Supplementary vol. 211–19.

Neurath, Otto, 131/2. "Sociology and Physicalism." 1959. In A. J. Ayer (ed.), *Logical Positivism*. New York: Free Press.

Pareto, Vilfredo, 1963. *The Mind and Society: A Treatise on General Sociology*. New York: Dover Publications.

Peters, R. S., 1958. *The Concept of Motivation*. New York: Humanities Press.

Popper, Karl R., 1964. *The Poverty of Historicism*. New York: Harper & Row.

————— 1970. "Reason or Revolution." *Archives Européenes de Sociologie* 11:252–62.

Putnam, Hilary, 1978. *Meaning and the Moral Sciences*. London: Routledge and Kegan Paul.

Quine, W. V. O., 1969. *Ontological Relativity and Other Essays*. New York: Columbia University Press.

Rosen, Jacqueline L. and Bernice Neugarten, 1960. "Ego Functions in the Middle and Later Years: A Thematic Apperception Study of Normal Adults." *Journal of Gerontology* 15:62–67.

Rubinstein, David, forthcoming. *Marx and Wittgenstein: Social Praxis and Social Explanation*. London: Routledge and Kegan Paul.

Ryan, Alan, 1970. *The Philosophy of the Social Sciences*. New York: Pantheon.

Scheffler, Israel, 1969. *The Anatomy of Inquiry*. New York: Alfred A. Knopf.

Schelling, Thomas, 1969. "Models of Segregation." *American Economic Review* 54:488–93.

Schutz, Alfred, 1967. *The Phenomenology of the Social World*. Evanston, Ill.: Northwestern University Press.

Spiro, Melford E., 1966. "Religion: Problems of Definition and Explanation," in M. Banton (ed.), *Anthropological Approaches to the Study of Religion*. London: Tavistock Publications.

Strauss, Leo, 1953. *Natural Right and History*. Chicago: University of Chicago Press.

Street, David P. and Eugene A. Weinstein, 1975. "Problems and Prospects of Applied Sociology." *American Sociologist* 10:65–72.

Taylor, Charles, 1964. *The Explanation of Behavior*. New York: Humanities Press.

Turner, Stephen, 1974. "Getting Clear about the Sign-Rule." *Sociological Quarterly* 15:571–88.

    1977. "Blau's Theory of Differentiation: Is It Explanatory?" *Sociological Quarterly* 18: 17–32.

    1979. "Translating Ritual Beliefs." *Philosophy of the Social Sciences* 9:401–23.

Turner, Stephen and David Carr, 1978. "The Process of Criticism in Interpretive Sociology and History." *Human Studies* 1:138–52.

Turner, Stephen and Daryl Chubin, 1979. "Chance and Eminence in Science." *Social Science Information* 18:437–49.

Turner, Stephen and Regis Factor, 1977. "The Critique of Positivist Sociology in Leo Strauss and Jürgen Habermas." *Sociological Analysis and Theory* 7:185–206.

Weber, Max, 1947. *The Theory of Social and Economic Organization*. trans. by A. M. Henderson and Talcott Parsons. New York: Free Press.

    1949. *The Methodology of Social Science*. Trans. by E. A. Shils and H. A. Finch. Glencoe, Ill.: Free Press.

Wellmer, Albrecht, 1970. "Empirico-Analytical and Critical Social Science." *Continuum* 8:12–26.

Winch, Peter, 1958. *The Idea of a Social Science and Its Relation to Philosophy*. New York: Humanities Press.

    1964. "Understanding a Primitive Society." *American Philosophical Quarterly* 1:307–24.

Wittgenstein, Ludwig, 1956. *Remarks on the Foundations of Mathematics*. London: Basil Blackwell.

    1958. *Philosophical Investigations*. 2nd ed. New York: Macmillan.

Index